YOUNG VIC
THEATRE COMPANY

BARCLAYS Stage

Partners *with* THE ARTS COUNCIL OF ENGLAND

Young Vic Theatre Company
IN ASSOCIATION WITH
WARWICK ARTS CENTRE & DARREN OCKERT PRODUCTIONS PRESENT

Arabian
Nights

adapted and directed by
DOMINIC COOKE

D0171729

YOUNG VIC THEATRE COMPANY

The Young Vic Theatre Company brings new versions of classic stories and seminal plays to audiences of all ages and backgrounds. Committed to making theatre available to all, we actively cultivate new audiences and integrate our productions with extensive off-stage work with partners in education and the community.

Our main auditorium is one of London's most adaptable spaces and is used to great effect to house a wide range of new works by outstanding artists: from magical adaptations of stories such as Arabian Nights and Grimm Tales to uncompromising new versions of Genet and Shakespeare. The Young Vic Studio is one of London's most important homes of experimental new theatre. Leading companies present work that subverts, questions and reflects contemporary life.

Teaching others about theatre, and learning ourselves from this activity, is integral to the Young Vic Theatre Company. We provide young people with the practical means to explore theatre through the skills and experience of our award-winning core creative team.

In recognition of our national and international reputation, we take our work beyond this theatre to audiences throughout Britain and across the world. We invite other leading theatre companies, who share our approaches to theatre, to bring their work to audiences at the Young Vic.

Young Vic Theatre Company
66 The Cut, South Bank, London SE1 8LZ
A company limited by guarantee, registered in England No.1188209
VAT Registration No: 236 673348. Charity Registration No: 268876

Box Office **0171 928 6363**
Administration **0171 633 0133**
Press Office **0171 620 0568** Fax **0171 928 1585**
email **info@youngvic.org**
website **www.youngvic.org**

Artistic Director **Tim Supple**
Administrative Producer **Caroline Maude**

Arts for Everyone

In September 1997, the Young Vic was awarded one of the highest National Lottery Arts for Everyone (A4E) awards in the country, which enables the company to implement a number of initiatives crucial to its future development:

- **A significant and integrated growth of the Young Vic's audience development programme (The Funded Ticket Scheme) into one of the largest audience development access projects ever seen;**

- **The development of a permanent company of actors and musicians to create new shows with longer rehearsal periods and higher production values;**

- **The encouragement of young artists on the cutting edge of performance to develop their work through experimentation in the Young Vic's award-winning Studio;**

- **A substantial and significant increase in the Young Vic's acclaimed work with teachers, schools, colleges and young people.**

A4E projects will run until 2001 and are certain to evolve, providing more opportunities to enjoy and participate in the world of theatre.

To realise the enormous potential that this award promises, the Young Vic must find companies, trusts and individuals who share in its commitment to this programme of work. Over the next three years, the Young Vic must raise a total of £100,000 in partnership funding to release this remarkable lottery award. We take this opportunity to acknowledge the support of **Allied Domecq plc** in providing a much needed lead gift of £36,000 over three years, together with the generous support of **David and Maria Willetts, The Royal Victoria Hall Foundation, J Sainsbury plc, Direct Connection, 3i Trustee Company Ltd, Shell International Ltd** and **The McKenna Charitable Trust.**

The Young Vic Funded Ticket Scheme (main sponsor Allied Domecq plc) provides an introduction to theatre for thousands of people of all ages who otherwise may not have attended, because of financial or social restraints. The scheme was created in 1994 to enable local school children, based on need, to visit the theatre for the first time, and now, due to the successful application to the National Lottery's Arts for Everyone programme, the Funded Ticket Scheme has been one of the Young Vic programmes to radically expand.

The New Funded Ticket Scheme, now in its second year, brought close to 10,000 new theatre-goers to the Young Vic during year one. If you would like further information regarding this scheme for a group within London and the home counties, contact the Audience Development Officer on **0171 633 0133**.

The Young Vic would like to express its sincere thanks to the many companies, foundations and private contributors who recognise the value of the company's work. These include:

Abbey National Charitable Trust Limited
Allied Domecq plc
Barclays Bank plc
Barclays Life Assurance Company Ltd
Beechdean Dairies Ltd
Thomas Bendhem
The Berkeley Group plc
British Steel plc
Calouste Gulbenkian Foundation
The D'Oyly Carte Charitable Trust
David Cohen Family Charitable Trust
David S Smith Holdings plc
The Eric Evans Memorial Trust
The Robert Gavron Charitable Trust
The Worshipful Company of Grocers
The Guardian Royal Exchange Charitable Trust
Mrs Margaret Guido's Charitable Trust
The Haberdashers' Company
Sue Hammerson's Charitable Trust
Help a London Child
Imperial Chemical Industries plc
John Lewis Partnership plc
Mathilda and Terence Kennedy Charitable Trust
Konditor & Cook
Corporation of London
The Lynn Foundation
Mr H A Molins
Marks and Spencer plc
The Peter Minet Trust
The Peter Moores Foundation
Newcomen Collett Foundation
The Persula Foundation
PriceWaterhouseCoopers

Railtrack plc
The Rayne Foundation
The Reuter Foundation
Royal and Sun Alliance Insurance Group plc
Sir Walter St John's Educational Charity
St Olave's and St Saviour's Grammar School Foundation
Simon's Charity
Snipe Charitable Trust
South West Trains Limited
The Stanley Foundation Ltd
TimeOut KidsOut Magazine
Garfield Weston Foundation
The Whitbread 1988 Charitable Trust
The Harold Hyam Wingate Foundation
The Woodward Charitable Trust

The Young Vic gratefully acknowledges a French Theatre Season Award for research into French Theatre
The Young Vic on the World Wide Web is supported by Direct Connection

The Young Vic gratefully acknowledges the financial assistance of the London Arts Board, London Boroughs Grants, the London Borough of Lambeth, the London Borough of Southwark, and the National Lottery, issued through the Arts Council of England.

Arabian Nights

This tour is made possible by BARCLAYS STAGE PARTNERS
a sponsorship scheme from Barclays and the Arts Council of England.

VENUE	DATE	BOX OFFICE NUMBER
Oxford Playhouse	5-14 August	01865 798 600
Edinburgh Assembly Rooms	17-30 August	0131 226 2428
Newcastle Theatre Royal	7-11 September	0191 232 2061
Billingham Forum	14-18 September	01652 552 663
Mold Theatr Clwyd	21-25 September	01352 755 114
Eastbourne Devonshire Park	5-9 October	01323 412 000
Dublin Olympia	12-16 October	0671 2860
Chatham Central Theatre	19-23 October	01634 403 868
Cheltenham Everyman	26-30 October	01242 572 573
Crawley The Hawth	3-6 November	01293 553 636
Glasgow Theatre Royal	9-13 November	0141 332 9000
Cork Opera House	16-20 November	00 353 (0)21 270 022
Warwick Arts Centre	7-24 December	01203 524 524

Arabian Nights

PERFORMERS IN ALPHABETICAL ORDER:

Natasha Gordon
Tracy Harper
Jonny Hoskins
Nicholas Khan
Tristan Sharps

Rohan Siva
Harmage Singh Kalirai
Sharlene Whyte
Yasmin Wilde

MUSICIANS

Damien Manning

Rebecca Austen-Brown

Adapted and Directed by	**Dominic Cooke**
Designed by	**Georgia Sion**
Music Composed by	**Gary Yershon**
Movement Director	**Liz Ranken**
Lighting Design by	**Paul Anderson**
Sound Designed by	**Crispian Covell**
	for Aura Sound Design Limited
Illusions by	**Paul Kieve**
Assistant Director	**Thea Sharrock**
Company & Stage Manager	**Katie Beedham**
Deputy Stage Manager	**Caroline Healey**
Assistant Stage Manager	**Sarah Braybrook**
Costume Supervisor	**Sarah Bowern**
Sound Technician	**Kooney John Vangeene**
General Management	**Darren Ockert**
	for Darren Ockert Productions
Production Management	**Phil Cameron**
	and Richard Blacksell
	for Background Production Limited
Tour Marketing and Press	**Tei Williams Tel: 01865 883139**

Production Acknowledgements

Set built by Warwick Arts Centre Workshops and Andy Beauchamp Scenery Construction. Tour arrangements by The Booking Office Tel: 0171 387 1555. Puppets made by Lucy Turner. Puppetry consultant Ronnie Le Drew. Props made by Paul Williams, Paul Gallagher and Anna Goller (work placement from Ohio University). Cloaks made by Helen Charlton. Costumes made by Judith Adams, Claire Boyle, Claire-Louise Hardie and Maria Rainsdern. Hats made by Mark Wheeler. With special thanks to Mandy Burnett and Patrick Anwyl for small props. Lighting equipment supplied by Sparks Theatrical Hire. Magic Bird by Anna Ingleby.

With thanks to:
Ruth Patron and Rebecca Chippendale (design assistants)
Craig Higginson, for programme material.
The Islamic Cultural Centre
Persil, Comfort and Stergene, courtesy of Lever Brothers, for Wardrobe Care.

First Performed at the Young Vic Theatre on **16 November 1998**
This touring production first perfromed at The Oxford Playhouse on **6 August 1999**

STORIES AND CHARACTERS

THE STORY OF SHAHRAYAR AND SHAHRAZAD

Shahrazad . . . .**Sharlene Whyte**
Dinarzad . . . .**Natasha Gordon**
Vizier . . . .**Tristan Sharps**
Shahrayar . . . .**Nicholas Khan**

THE STORY OF ALI BABA AND THE FORTY THIEVES

Ali Baba . . . .**Rohan Siva**
Kasim/Ali Baba's Son **Jonny Hoskins**
Ali Baba's Wife . . .**Natasha Gordon**
Kasim's Wife . . . .**Yasmin Wilde**
Captain Of The Forty Thieves
. . . .**Tristan Sharps**
Marjana . . . .**Tracy Harper**
Baba Mustapha
. . . .**Harmage Singh Kalirai**

THE STORY OF THE LITTLE BEGGAR

Tailor . . . .**Rohan Siva**
Tailor's Wife/Hangman
. . . .**Natasha Gordon**
Beggar . . . .**Jonny Hoskins**
Doctor's Maid/Merchant
. . . .**Tracy Harper**
Doctor . . . .**Tristan Sharps**
Doctor's Wife . . . . . .**Yasmin Wilde**
Steward . . .**Harmage Singh Kalirai**
Chief Of Police . . . .**Sharlene Whyte**

THE ADVENTURE OF ES-SINDIBAD OF THE SEA

Es-Sindibad The Porter
. . . .**Jonny Hoskins**
Es-Sindibad The Sailor
. . . .**Tristan Sharps**
Page . . . .**Natasha Gordon**

HOW ABU HASSAN BROKE WIND

Abu Hassan
. . . .**Harmage Singh Kalirai**
Marriage Broker/Girl . . . .
. . . .**Yasmin Wilde**
Bride . . . .**Natasha Gordon**

THE STORY OF THE WIFE WHO WOULDN'T EAT

Amina . . . .**Tracy Harper**
Sidi Nu'uman 1 . . . .**Rohan Siva**
Sidi Nu'uman 2 . . . . .**Jonny Hoskins**
Haroun Al-Rashid . .**Tristan Sharps**
Baker . . . . .**Harmage Singh Kalirai**
Good Sorceress' Mother
. . . .**Sharlene Whyte**
Good Sorceress . . .**Natasha Gordon**

THE STORY OF THE ENVIOUS SISTERS

Khusrau Shah . . . . .**Nicholas Khan**
Khusrau Shah's Vizier/Wise Old Man
. . . .**Tristan Sharps**
Eldest Sister/Old Religious Woman
. . . .**Tracy Harper**
Middle Sister/Steward's Wife
. . . .**Yasmin Wilde**
Youngest Sister . . . .**Sharlene Whyte**
Khusrau Shah's Steward/Cook
. . . .**Harmage Singh Kalirai**
Bahman . . . .**Jonny Hoskins**

Perviz . . . .**Rohan Siva**
Parizade . . . .**Natasha Gordon**

Other parts played by members of the company

BIOGRAPHIES

PAUL ANDERSON *Lighting Designer*

Work includes *Special Occasions*, *Hospitality*, *A Coupla White Chicks Sitting Around Talking* (for North American Theatre in the UK), *Real World* (Soho Poly - Sandpiper Productions), *The Double Bass* (The Man in the Moon), *West Side Story*, *Guys and Dolls*, *Twelfth Night*, *As I Lay Dying* and the original production of *Arabian Nights* (Young Vic), *Cinderella* (Theatre Royal Stratford East), *Two Seasons of Orangeries* (Academia Italiana – displays of Italian fine art), *Rediscovering Pompei* (IBM exhibition), re-lights of *The Street Of Crocodiles*, *The Three Lives of Lucie Cabrol* (Theatre de Complicite), re-lights of *The Caucasian Chalk Circle* (RNT/Theatre de Complicite), *The Chairs* (Theatre de Complicite/Royal Court – nominee for the 1998 Olivier, Drama Desk, and Tony Award), *Mnemonic* (Theatre de Complicite).

DOMINIC COOKE *Director*

Theatre includes original production of *Arabian Nights* (Young Vic), *Hunting Scenes from Lower Bavaria*, *The Weavers* (Gate Theatre), *Afore Night Come*, *Entertaining Mr Sloane* (Theatre Clwyd), *The Bullet* (Donmar Warehouse), *My Mother Said I Never Should* (Oxford Stage Company), *Of Mice and Men* (Nottingham Playhouse), *Kiss of the Spiderwoman* (Bolton Octagon), *Autogeddon* (Edinburgh Assembly Rooms – Fringe First), *The Marriage of Figaro* (tour, adaptation and direction – winner of the Manchester Evening News Award). Assistant Director at the Royal Shakespeare Company, 1992 – 1994. Currently Associate Director of the Royal Court Theatre.

NATASHA GORDON *Performer*

Trained at Guildhall, this is her professional debut in theatre. Television includes *The Bill*, *The Cone Zone* (Thames Television).

TRACY HARPER *Performer*

Theatre includes *Ion*, *Tambourlaine*, *The Odyssey* (RSC), *Mutiny* (Piccadilly Theatre), *Aladdin and World Stories* (Stratford East), *Blood Wedding* (Half Moon Theatre), *Wind in the Willows* (The Old Vic), *The Magicolympic Games* (Royal National Theatre). Toured with The Half Moon, Oxford Stage Company, Royal National Theatre. Film includes Lolita in *The Sender* (Paramount Films), *Madness Museum* (for Ken Campbell Channel Four Films), *Unfair Exchange* (BBC1), *Pillowbook* (for Peter Greenaway). Radio includes *Macbeth*, *Gunchester* (BBC). Television includes *Split Ends*, *First Among Equals* (Granada), *Dempsey and Makepeace* (LWT), *Casualty* (BBC).

JONNY HOSKINS *Perfomer*

Theatre includes *Peter Pan* (Royal National Theatre), *King Ubu* (Gate Theatre), *Marie and Lizzie* (Contact Theatre Manchester), *Aesop's Fables* (Savoy Theatre), *Metamorphoses* (The Clod Ensemble), *Grease* (Theatre in the Mill), *Street Creatures* (The Stockton Riverside Festival), *The Water Children* (National Theatre Studio), *The Canterbury Tales* (Alive & Kicking, European Tour), *The Knack, Plunder* (for the NT2000 celebrations at The Royal National Theatre). Film includes *Jealousy* and *Nocturnal.*

NICHOLAS KHAN *Performer*

Theatre includes *The Lion the Witch and the Wardrobe, The Winter's Tale* (Royal Shakespeare Company), *Animal Crackers* (Manchester Royal Exchange), Mose in *Egitto* (Royal Opera House), *Catherine* (King's Head Theatre), *Blood Wedding* (Cockpit), *Sawn-Off Shakespeare* (Riverside Studio, Edinburgh, Seattle), *MAA!* (Royal Court), *Wigs of Wonderment* (ICA), *Dick Whittington, Aladdin, Jack and The Beanstalk, Ali Baba and The Forty Thieves, The Wonderland Adventures of Alice* (Bubble Theatre Company). *Brave New World* (Cochrane Theatre). Film includes *Star Wars – The Phantom Menace*.

PAUL KIEVE *Illusionist*

A Gold Star member of the Inner Magic Circle, theatre work includes *The Invisible Man* (Stratford East and West End), *Haroun and the Sea of Stories, La Grande Magia,* (Royal National Theatre), *Blithe Spirit* (Chichester), *Cinderella* with Improbable (Lyric Hammersmith), *Into the Woods* (Donmar), *Grimm Tales* (New York), *Alice In Wonderland* (English National Ballet – Coliseum), *The Witches* (Duke of Yorks, Vaudeville), *Scrooge, The Musical* (Dominion), *The Treatment, Tantamount Esperence* (Royal Court), *A Passionate Woman* (Comedy), *The Tempest , The Strange Case of Dr Jekyll and Mr Hyde, Spring Awakening,* (RSC). Opera includes *Parsifal* (Paris), *Macbeth* (Hamburg), *La Calisto* (Batignano), *Elixir of Love* (E.N.O). Consultancy work with *David Copperfield, Orlan* (I.C.A.), *Andrew Lloyd Webber*. Television includes *The Ronn Lucas Show, Tricks And Tracks, New Faces, Good Stuff, David Copperfield Show.*

LIZ RANKEN *Movement Director*

Work as a Movement Director includes *House of Bernada Alba, Anna Karenina* -Time Out Award, *The Mill On The Floss, Jane Eyre, War and Peace, The Tempest* (Shared Experience), *The Changeling,*

Triolus and Cressida, Midsummer Nights Dream, Richard III, As You Like It (RSC), *My Mother Said I Never Should* (Oxford Stage Company), *Hunting Scenes form Lower Bavaria, The Weavers* (Gate Theatre), *Twelfth Night* (Sailsbury Playhouse). *DV8* physical theatre, *CAT A* (in prisons and theatres). Film includes choreographer for feature film *Alive & Kicking*, BBC2 Dance for Camera *Touched* choreographer/performer. As a director/performer *Summat-a-do-wi-weddins* (won Plays Portfolio Choreographic award), *Funk off Green* (won Capital Award Edinburgh Fringe), *Ooh* (3rd Eye Glasgow with performers with and without disability).

TRISTAN SHARPS *Performer*

Trained at Jacques Lecoq. Theatre includes *Richard III* (English Shakespeare Company). *Treasure Island* (Lyric Hammersmith), *Things Fall Apart* (Royal Court/Lift), *A Perfect Ganesh, The Hypochondriac and Le Medecin Volant* (West Yorkshire Playhouse), *Custer's Last Stand* (Sailsbury Playhouse), *Death in Venice, Crime and Punishmnet* (Red Shift), *Liars, Fakers* (Talking Pictures), *The Duchess of Malfi* (Pint Blank), *Musical Scenes* (Clod Ensemble) British Council Tour to Czech Republic), *Vesalius: A Requiem* (BCT to Italy), *2000* (Shaker Productions), *Obsession and Hatchet Plan* (La Compagnie du Partis-Pris), *Adrian Mole* (Act/Paris), *Ubu* (RNT Studio). Directing Credits include: *Loves Labours Lost* (Sharp Edge), *Bye Bye, Mr Y* (Shaker Productions), and as Movement director *King Ubu* (The Gate). Film includes: *Mr Frost, The Launch.* Television includes: *The Canterville Ghost.*

THEA SHARROCK *Assistant Director*

As assistant director theatre includes *Salome* (Riverside Studios), *Intimate Death* (Gate Theatre), *Don Juan* (English Touring Theatre). Before University Thea worked at the Market Theatre Johannesberg and as Assistant to the Head of the Royal National Theatre Studio. She has been a member of the Anna Scher Theatre for over twelve years.

HAMARGE SINGH KALIRAI *Performer*

Theatre includes original production of *Arabian Nights* (Young Vic), *Bravely Fought the Queen* (Border Crossing), *Riddley Walker, The Moonstone* (The Royal Exchange Manchester), *My Beautiful Laundrette* (The Sherman Cardiff), *Dick Whittington* (The Grand Wolverhampton), *The Illusion* (The Old Vic), *Passage to India* (The Redgrave Farnham), *Doolaly Days* (The Haymarket Leicester), Films include *Guru in Seven* (Balhar), *Brothers in Trouble* (Renegade), *Paper Mask* (Granada), *Partition* (Bandung), *A Very British Coup*

(Skerba). Television Credits include *The Cops* (World), *Trial and Retribution* (La Plante), *A Touch of Frost* (YTV), *Hearts and Minds, Lovejoy* (Witzend), *Medics* (Granada), *The Knock* (Bronson Knight), *The Bill* (Thames), *Family Pride* (Central*), The Good Guys* (LWT).

GEORGIA SION *Designer*

Theatre includes original production of *Arabian Nights* (Young Vic), *The Cosmonaut's Last Message…, Crave, Sleeping Around* (Paines Plough), *Perfect Days* (Traverse, Hampstead, Vaudeville Theatre), *Caravan* (National Theatre of Norway), *Afore Night Come* (Theatre Clwyd), *The Weavers* (Costume- Gate Theatre), *Twelfth Night* (Central School of Speech and Drama), *Othello* (Watermill Theatre, Tokyo Globe), *The sunset Ship* (Young Vic), *Lovers* (RSC Fringe Festival). Opera includes: *A Medicine for Melancholy, A-Ronne* (ENO Bayliss Programme), *Four Saints in Three Acts* (Trinity Opera), *King and Marshal* (Bloomsbury Theatre).

ROHAN SIVA *Performer*

Trained at RADA, theatre includes *The Ragged Child* (NYMT), *The Island, My Children! My Africa* (Edinburgh Fringe). This is Rohan's professional debut.

YASMIN WILDE *Performer*

Theatre includes the original production of *Arabian Nights* (Young Vic), *The Jungle Book, Arabian Nights* (Midlands Arts Centre), *Heavenly Bodies* (Leicester Haymarket), *Shakers* (Hull Truck Theatre – UK tour), *The Jungle Book* (Manchester Library Theatre – UK tour), *Romeo and Juliet* (Orange Tree Theatre – UK tour), *Yerma* (Southwark Playhouse), *Dancing in the Street, Summer in the City* (DGM Productions). Television includes *Teenage Health Freak* Channel 4 *The Bill* (Thames Television).

GARY YERSHON *Composer*

Theatre includes *Don Carlos, The Unexpected Man, Hamlet, The Merchant of Venice, Artists and Admirers, As You Like It, The Virtuoso, The Devil is an Ass* (RSC), *Troilus and Cressida, The Way of the World, Volpone, Broken Glass, The Tempest, Pericles* (RNT), *Death of a Salesman, Peter Pan, A Perfect Ganesh, The Government Inspector* (West Yorkshire Playhouse), *Medea, The School for Scandal, Death and the King's Horseman, The Winter's Tale, Julius Caesar, Tartuffe* (Manchester Royal Exchange), original production of *Arabian Nights, Miss Julie, The Iron Man, The Winter's Tale* (Young Vic). As musical director *Topsy-Turvy* (for Mike Leigh), and *The*

Threepenny Opera (Donmar Warehouse). Radio includes Pushkin's *Ruslan and Lyudmila* (for Radio 3 – as translator/dramatist). Television includes the children's cartoon series - *James The Cat* and *Painted Tales*.

SHARLENE WHYTE *Performer*
Trained at RADA, theatre includes *Guiding Light* (Warwick House). TV includes *As If*, Carnival Films. This is Sharlene's professional debut since graduating.

Arabian Nights

The folk tales which have collectively survived as *The Thousand and One Nights* are of Indian, Persian, and Arabic origin. Many of the stories were circulated orally for centuries before being written down.

The first records that the tales existed orally come to us via Arab historians from the tenth century. It was only by the latter half of the thirteenth century, however, that the different manuscripts of the tales began to emerge in written form. During the eighteenth century, the first European translations began to appear, influencing writers such as Rousseau and the English Romantics, and became as much a part of Western culture as Eastern. However, Eastern scholars were reluctant to give these irreverent stories the 'classic' status they were achieving for themselves in the West.

Since the thirteenth century, there have been many versions of *The Thousand and One Nights,* mainly from Egypt and Syria. Most recent scholarship claims a fourteenth century Syrian manuscript as the authentic text, but no doubt there will be others who disagree.

What endures over and above these academic debates is the strange power of the tales themselves, with their depiction of a unique world of supernatural forces and fabulous wealth, juxtaposed with the basic physical conditions and deep-rooted psychological needs of ordinary people, whether they be medieval or contemporary, Islamic or Christian, young or old.

Craig Higginson

ARABIAN NIGHTS COLLABORATORS

The *Arabian Nights* tour is organised by the Young Vic Theatre Company, Warwick Arts Centre and Darren Ockert Productions, with funding from Barclays Stage Partners, a sponsorship scheme from Barclays and the Arts Council of England

Warwick Arts Centre

Arabian Nights is one of the highlights of Warwick Arts Centre's 25th Birthday Year. At the heart of the University of Warwick campus and only 3 miles from Coventry city centre, Warwick Arts Centre presents the broadest range of the highest quality events in the Midlands region and is the largest complex if its kind outside London.

Last year over 230,000 visits were made to over 1,300 different events. These ranged from classic drama to experimental theatre; standup comedy to rock and pop; film screenings and visual arts to contemporary dance; classical music and opera to family shows and a leading literature programme. In fact there's something for everyone - and all under one roof.
Stay in touch and visit our web site at www.warwick.ac.uk/ArtsCentre.

Darren Ockert Productions

Darren Ockert Productions is an independent production company based at the Young Vic Theatre in London. It was established in January 1997 and aims to promote new and exciting works and talent.

The company has experience of producing and touring family shows: *The Canterville Ghost,* starring Ron Moody toured the UK to No. 1 national venues in 1998. Previous Christmas shows based on quality works and involving community participation and audience development included *The Little Match Girl* at Trinity Arts Centre. Two new shows are in development - *The Snow Queen* and *Jason and the Argonauts* - for 2000. New works commissioned by the company include *Three Lost Souls* (BAC and the Kings Head) and *Theatrical Love* (Wimbledon), and the most recent production is *Scooter Thomas Makes It To The Top of the World* also at Wimbledon. The company is currently working on a musical version of the classic horror film *Theatre of Blood*, which starred Vincent Price and Diana Rigg. This is scheduled for a West End opening in late autumn 2000.

ARABIAN NIGHTS

adapted by
Dominic Cooke

For Aoife

Setting

An empty space with two areas: one for storytelling and one for listening.

Cast

The original production called for a company of nine. The
parts could happily be played by the same or more actors and
distributed differently. It is essential that Shahrayar is listening,
and not participating in the first few stories and preferable that
there is some resonance between the casting of 'The Story of
the Envious Sisters' and the frame story. At the Young Vic the
parts were cast as follows:

Chu Omambala   Shahravar/Great (Abu Hassan)/Ghoul
(Wife Who Wouldn't Eat)/Khosrou Shah

Tim McMullen   Vizier/Captain of the Forty Thieves/Doctor/
Es-Sindibad the Sailor/Haroun al-Fashid/Vizier (Envious
Sisters)/Wise Old Man

Peter Bailie   Masud/Ali Baba/Little Beggar/Sidi 2/Baker
(Envious Sisters)/Perviz

Harmage Singh Kalirai   Headsman/Baba Mustapha/
Steward/Abu Hassan/Baker (Wife Who Wouldn't Eat)/Steward
(Envious Sisters)

Paul Chahidi   Kasim/Ali Baba's Son/Tailor/Watchman/
Es-Sindibad the Porter/Sidi 1/1st Cook/Bahman

Sophie Okonedo   Shahrazad/Chief of Police/Good Sorceress/
Youngest Sister/Talking Bird

Kate Fleetwood   Dinarzad/Kasim's Wife/Tailor's Wife/
Hangman/Page/2nd Customer/Parizade

Yasmin Wilde   Ali Baba's Wife/Doctor's Wife/King (Little Beggar) 1st Customer/Second Sister

Ishia Bennison   Shahrayar's First Wife/Marjanah/Merchant (Little Beggar)/Amina /Eldest Sister/Old Religious Woman

Merchants in Es-Sindibad, Guests at Abu Hassan's wedding, dogs and other parts played by members of the company.

Prologue

SHAHRAZAD. Long long ago, in a faraway land, there lived a
clever young girl called Shahrazad.

DINARZAD. She lived with her little sister who was called
Dinarzad . . .

VIZIER. . . . . and her father who was the Vizier, the chief
adviser to the King.

The Vizier loved both his daughters very much.

A family grouping.

DINARZAD. Dinarzad was as kind, loyal and true as any girl
her age.

SHAHRAZAD. But Shahrazad was courageous, shrewd and
bright well beyond her years.

And there was nothing she liked better than to read stories.

DINARZAD. Stories of enchanted caves . . .

SHAHRAZAD. . . . . of flesh eating ghouls . . .

DINARZAD. . . . . of talking birds . . .

SHAHRAZAD. . . . . flying men . . .

DINARZAD. Night after night, she would keep her little sister
awake by filling her head with these stories.

Dinarzad lies in bed with the covers pulled up high.
Shahrazad sits at the end of the bed. She is in the middle of
telling a terrifying story.

SHAHRAZAD. When suddenly the huge bird dropped him in
a valley of slimy tree-sized snakes.

Dinarzad screams.

VIZIER (*enters*). It's getting very late, children, you must get to sleep.

DINARZAD. Please father, please let Shahrazad finish.

SHAHRAZAD. We're near the end now.

VIZIER. Very well then. The end of the story. Then bed.

SHAHRAZAD. However many times she told these stories, she never forgot a word, for Shahrazad was gifted with a perfect memory.

SHAHRAYAR. Now the King of this country was called Shahrayar.

QUEEN. He lived with a beautiful wife that he loved as he loved his own eyes.

Another family grouping. They dance together, romantically.

SHAHRAYAR. Shahrayar was a great leader; courageous, big hearted and strong. By his enemies he was feared but by his people he was loved.

VIZIER. And the halls of the palace would sing with his laughter.

We see the laughing King.

SHAHRAYAR. One day Shahrayar was at the Palace window overlooking the garden, when a secret door opened.

Shahrayar watches as his wife, the queen, comes out, She looks around.

QUEEN. Masud, Masud!

A slave jumps from a tree and rushes to her. They dance very sensually together.

SHAHRAYAR. I trusted my wife as I trusted the ground beneath my feet. No man is safe in the world. Curse the World, curse Life and curse all Women!

VIZIER. Now the King is strengthened by his Vizier as the body is by the back.

SHAHRAYAR. Shahrayar went to the Vizier and said to him:

Take that wife of mine and put her to death.

VIZIER. The Vizier did this, for if he disobeyed the King's will he would be killed himself.

SHAHRAYAR. The gates of the King's heart were locked like a prison . . .

VIZIER. . . . and the halls of the palace were as silent as a tomb.

SHAHRAYAR. The King swore that from now on he would marry for one night only,

A stilted wedding dance.

and the next morning . . .

VIZIER. . . . ordered the Vizier to have the Executioner cut off his wife's head.

SHAHRAYAR. He continued to do this for a thousand nights . . .

WOMEN. . . . till a thousand young girls perished . . .

SHAHRAYAR. . . . and every morning he would say to himself:

There is not a single good woman anywhere on the face of the earth.

SHAHRAZAD. By now, Shahrazad had grown up into a wise, refined, and beautiful young woman.

DINARZAD. Dinarzad had grown up too!

VIZIER. One day the Vizier returned home from the palace with his head weighed down with worry.

SHAHRAZAD. Why are you looking so lost, Father?

VIZIER. It seems the sun has set on our city forever. Mothers and daughters are fleeing in fear. And those that are left behind are locked up in their houses. Today I passed the mosque and saw hundreds of shoes lined up outside. Not one pair was a woman's.

SHAHRAZAD. Father, I have a favour to ask and hope that you will grant me it.

VIZIER. I will not refuse it. If it is just and reasonable.

SHAHRAZAD. I have a plan to save the daughters of the city.

VIZIER. Your aim, daughter is admirable but King Shahrayar's sickness is beyond help. How could you hope to cure it?

SHAHRAZAD. I want you to marry me to the King.

Silence.

I mean it father. I want you to marry me to him. Today.

VIZIER. Have you lost your mind, daughter? You know what happens in the Palace every morning . . .

SHAHRAZAD. I know that father. I am not afraid.

VIZIER. When the king orders me to send you to the executioner, I must obey. I, your father, will have your blood on my hands.

SHAHRAZAD. Father, you must trust me. Marry me to the king.

VIZIER. I forbid you to ever mention this again.

SHAHRAZAD. Either you take me, or I shall go myself. I will tell the King that I asked you to marry me to him and you refused. That you begrudged him your daughter and disobeyed his will.

VIZIER. Please think again, daughter. Don't do this.

SHAHRAZAD. I'm sorry father, I must.

VIZIER. May Allah not deprive me of you.

The Vizier prays.

SHAHRAZAD. Dinarzad, listen closely to what I have to say. When I go to the King, I will send for you to stay with me in the bridal chamber. When you come, remember to wake me an hour before daybreak and ask me to tell you a story.

DINARZAD. Sister, I will do all I can to help you.

VIZIER. At nightfall the Vizier led Shahrazad to the Palace of great King Shahrayar.

The King enters.

Shahrazad kisses the ground before the King.

A short strained wedding ritual dance.

SHAHRAYAR. Uncover your face.

Shahrazad removes her veil.

You are very beautiful.

Shahrazad starts crying.

Why are you crying?

SHAHRAZAD. I have a sister. I would like her to stay with me here tonight, so that I might say good-bye and enjoy her company one last time.

SHAHRAYAR. Shahrayar agreed and Dinarzad was sent for . . .

DINARZAD. . . . who came with all possible speed.

SHAHRAYAR. The King and Queen got into a bed raised very high . . .

DINARZAD. . . . and Dinarzad lay down on some cushions on the floor underneath.

An hour before daybreak, Dinarzad did as her sister asked.

Dinarzad clears her throat.

Sister, if you are not too sleepy, tell me one of your strange and wonderful stories to while away the night. For I don't know what will happen to you tomorrow.

SHAHRAZAD. May I have permission to tell a story, my Lord?

SHAHRAYAR. You may.

SHAHRAZAD. Very well.

Listen . . .

ACT ONE

The Story of Ali Baba and the Forty Thieves

In this story, the thieves are played as a chorus, becoming the horses, the cave, and the treasure inside.

SHAHRAZAD. In a city in Persia there lived two brothers. One called Kasim and the other Ali Baba. When he died, their father left them an equal share of his tiny fortune. But luck had not been half as fair. Kasim married a rich widow who owned a shop bursting with fine goods. He soon became a wealthy man and lived a life of ease. Ali Baba, on the other hand, married a woman as dirt poor as he was. He lived very sparsely and was forced to scratch a living chopping wood in a nearby forest and bringing it to sell in on two asses, which were all he owned in the world.

ALI BABA. One day, when Ali Baba was in the forest, he noticed, in the distance, a vast cloud of dust. When he looked closer he saw a band of horsemen riding towards him at great speed. Ali Baba was suspicious. He climbed a tall, close-leafed tree next to a cliff, where he could hide without being seen.

The horsemen enter. They are wearing black capes, armed with knives and carrying bulging saddle bags. Shaharazad joins them.

CAPTAIN. Dismount!

The thieves dismount.

ALI BABA. Ali Baba counted the men and found that they numbered forty. He guessed from their cold and black beards that they were bandits.

CAPTAIN. The one he took for their Captain passed under the tree and stood in front of the cliff.

The thieves become the cliff.

OPEN SESAME!

The cliff door opens. The Captain enters and also becomes the cliff.

ALI BABA. Immediately the door swept shut.

The door shuts.

Ali Baba froze in the tree for some time. Eventually, it opened again, and the forty thieves appeared.

CAPTAIN. CLOSE SESAME!

The door shuts.

SHAHRAZAD. Each thief mounted his horse and they galloped off into the dust.

Ali Baba climbs down and goes to the door.

ALI BABA. OPEN SESAME.

Instantly the door flies wide open. The thieves become the inside of the cliff by reversing their capes which are lined with gold.

Ali Baba was astonished to find a bright, airy cavern, carved out of the rock like the holy dome of a mosque. Inside was a landscape of limitless riches. Islands of sparkling treasure sat in rivers of rich silks and brocades, valleys of precious carpets and above all, mountain upon mountain of sacks and purses bursting with shimmering gold and silver coins.

He quickly gathered as many gold coins as his asses could carry.

ALI BABA. OPEN SESAME!

He stands before the door and gives the command.

ALI BABA. CLOSE SESAME!

At once the door shuts.

He covered the coins with firewood to prevent them being seen and set off for home.

ALI BABA. Wife, look what I have for you.

He puts the bags at her feet. His wife prods them, looks inside one. Then he empties the bags on to the floor, and the cascades of gold dazzle her eyes.

ALI'S WIFE. Ali Baba, How could you? We may be poor, but there's no need to steal.

ALI BABA. Shh wife, calm down and keep quiet. Wait till you hear what just happened.

He told her his adventures from beginning to end and they agreed to keep the whole story as secret as the mystery of the pyramids.

ALI'S WIFE (*screaming*). We're rich!

She does a little dance of joy and then starts to count the gold piece by piece.

ALI'S WIFE. One, two, three, four . . .

ALI BABA. Don't be a dolt, wife. It would take all week to get this lot counted. We need to hide the coins. This minute. I shall dig a hole in the garden.

ALI'S WIFE. No, it's no good. I simply have to know precisely how much we've got. I'll borrow some scales from the neighbours. I'll quickly weigh the gold while you dig the hole.

ALI BABA. Alright then. But remember: be on your guard.

ALI'S WIFE. Ali Baba's wife fluttered over to her brother-in-law Kasim's, who lived nearby. As he was not at home, she asked his wife if she would kindly lend her some scales for a short while.

KASIM'S WIFE. Certainly. Wait here while I fetch them.

Now, the sister-in-law knew how poor Ali Baba was, and was desperate to find out what they could be weighing. So she greased the inside of the pan of the scales.

Kasim's wife goes back and gives the scales to Ali Baba's wife.

I am sorry it's taken me so long. I just couldn't find them anywhere.

ALI'S WIFE. Ali Baba's wife took the scales home and began to weigh the gold. Whilst Ali Baba buried it, she returned them.

Sister-in-law, I said I would only be a while. I am as good as my word. Here they are. I am much obliged.

She exits. Kasim's wife peers into the scales and finds a piece of gold stuck to the pan.

KASIM'S WIFE. What is this? Ali Baba has enough gold to fill a pair of scales? Where did the penniless pauper get it from?

Enter Kasim.

Kasim, you think yourself rich, but you are mistaken, Ali Baba has far more money than you. He doesn't count his gold as you do. He weighs it.

Kasim's wife shows Kasim the gold coin.

KASIM. Instead of feeling happy for her brother's good fortune, Kasim was stricken with deadly jealousy. Before sunrise the next morning, he marched straight over to his brother's house.

He knocks on the door.

Ali Baba, my wife found this stuck to the scales you borrowed yesterday.

Kasim shows Ali Baba the coin.

I demand an explanation.

ALI BABA. Ali Baba realised that, thanks to his dozy wife, Kasim had discovered their secret. So rather than risking all the thieves gold, he struck a deal. He agreed to tell Kasim where he found the treasure, if Kasim would share it equally and promise never to tell a soul.

KASIM. At dawn the next day, Kasim set off with huge chests loaded onto ten mules.

Enter the thieves as mules.

He followed the directions Ali Baba had given till he reached the cliff.

The thieves become the cliff.

OPEN SESAME!

The door flies open. As he enters the thieves become the inside of the cave.

His eyes pored over the riches inside, which were far beyond his wildest dreams. Greed and longing so possessed him that he spent the day in open mouthed wonder, and clean forgot till evening that he had come to take some away.

At last he snapped out of his trance and dragged as many sacks as he could to the door.

OPEN SATSUMA!

The door remains closed.

OPEN SEMOLINA! . . . OPEN SULTANA! . . . OPEN SARDINE!

The stubborn door doesn't budge.

The more Kasim searched for the word, the more it escaped him.

Until the flame of his greed went out and froze into icy dread.

SHAHRAZAD. Toward midnight, the thieves returned to their cavern and noticed Kasim's mules grazing sleepily by the rock, loaded with empty trunks.

CAPTAIN. The Captain went directly to the door, his steely dagger glinting in his hand.

OPEN SESAME!

Kasim charges towards the door, the thieves surround him and kill him.

SHAHRAZAD. The thieves resolved to cut Kasim's body into quarters and display it inside the cavern, placing two pieces on one side of the door and two on the other. This would terrify anyone else who attempted to break in. Then, they mounted their horses, and set off to search the countryside for caravans to rob.

The thieves disappear.

KASIM'S WIFE (*to Ali Baba*). It's late and my husband hasn't come home and I'm terrified something bad has happened.

ALI BABA. After begging her to stay calm for the sake of secrecy, Ali Baba set off for the forest with his asses. When he approached the cliff, he saw no sign of his brother or the mules. But he did see a pool of blood by the door which chilled him to the bone.

He crept to the door and gave the command.

Ali Baba finds the quartered body.

Despite Kasim's coldness towards him, Ali Baba knew that, by Allah's law, his brother must be buried properly. So without hesitating, he found a cloth to wrap up the remains. Then, he loaded them onto his asses with three more sacks of gold and set off back to his brother's house in town.

Ali Baba knocks at the door.

MARJANAH. The door was opened by Marjanah, a clever slave-girl.

ALI BABA. Marjanah, my life depends on your secrecy. These two bundles contain your master's murdered body. Without raising any suspicion, we must bury him as if he died of natural causes. For if anyone suspects that he was murdered, his killers will come in search of me as his accomplice.

MARJANAH. First thing the next morning, Marjanah set off to visit a poor old cobbler on the market square called Baba Mustapha.

BABA. Because he was so penniless, he needed to work harder than anyone else and his shop was always the first to open.

MARJANAH. Good morning.

She places a gold coin in his hand.

Baba Mustapha, fetch your needle and thread and come with me quickly. But I must warn you, when we leave the town centre I shall blindfold you.

BABA. What are you up to? I don't like the sound of this. I've got my reputation to think about.

Marjanah put another gold coin in his hand.

MARJANAH. Your good name is safe in my hands. Just come with me and fear nothing.

BABA. Baba Mustapha followed Marjanah through the morning shadows, to the edge of the town centre.

She blindfolds him.

MARJANAH. She led him to Kasim's house, to the room where the quartered body lay.

She takes his blindfold off.

Baba Mustapha, I brought you here to sew the pieces of this body together. When you finish, I shall give you another piece of gold.

Baba Mustapha sews the four pieces into one. Marjanah gives Baba another coin. She then blindfolds him again.

Marjanah forced Baba Mustapha to swear an oath of secrecy. Then she led him back to the edge of the town centre.

She takes the blindfold off.

MARJANAH. When she returned, they carried Kasim's body to the cemetery.

SHAHRAZAD. And so the secret of Kasim's gruesome murder was locked away as tight as the clasp on a miser's purse. And no one in the city suspected a thing.

ALI BABA. Three days later, under the cloak of nightfall, Ali Baba . . .

ALI'S WIFE. . . . his wife . . .

ALI'S SON. . . . and their son . . .

ALI BABA. . . . carried their few belongings . . .

ALI'S WIFE. . . . with their gold . . .

ALI'S SON. . . . to Kasim's big house . . .

ALL THREE. . . . to live in wealth and splendour . . .

ALI BABA. Ali Baba gave Kasim's thriving shop to his son,

Ali Baba gives his son a key.

promising that if he managed it wisely, he would receive the key to greater riches when he married.

SHAHRAZAD. Let us leave Ali Baba to the fruits of his golden fortune and return to the forty thieves.

When they returned to their forest hideaway, they were astounded to find Kasim's body and several bags of gold missing.

CAPTAIN. Someone else knows the secret of the cave. We must act quickly or risk losing everything. I shall go down into the town and listen out for talk of a murdered man. I shall find out who he was and where he lived. When I find his accomplice we shall put him to a slow and lingering death.

Temptation

The King's room. Dawn.

The Captain freezes.

Sound of a sword being sharpened.

Enter the Vizier and Executioner.

VIZIER. The executioner awaits your command, your majesty.

DINARZAD. What an extraordinary story, sister. I would love to hear the rest of it.

SHAHRAZAD. You will never guess what happens next. I shall tell you tonight, if the King lets me live.

VIZIER. Your majesty?

SHAHRAZAD. Doesn't his majesty want to know if Ali Baba survives?

Pause.

Or whether the cunning slave girl outwits the Captain of the forty thieves?

Pause. Shahrayar is torn.

SHAHRAYAR. Vizier, come back tomorrow. At the same time.

VIZIER. Certainly, your majesty.

Shahrazad, Dinarzad and Vizier share a moment of relief.

SHAHRAZAD. The day melted into night.

DINARZAD. And an hour before dawn, Dinarzad said:

Sister, if you are not too sleepy, tell the rest of your strange and wonderful story.

SHAHRAZAD. May I have your permission to continue the story, my Lord?

SHAHRAYAR. Yes.

SHAHRAZAD. Very well.

Listen . . .

The Story of Ali Baba and the Forty Thieves continues

SHAHRAZAD. The captain of the forty thieves disguised himself and set off, arriving in the city at daybreak.

SHAHRAZAD *and* CAPTAIN. He walked and walked . . .

CAPTAIN. . . . until he came to the first shop he saw open.

BABA. It was the shabby shop of Baba Mustapha.

Baba Mustapha sits with a needle in his hand, sewing a shoe.

CAPTAIN. Good morning old man. You start work very early. Is it possible that at your fine old age you have such good eyesight?

BABA. You do not know me. I may be old as the crumbling earth, but I still have perfect eyes. Not long ago, in a place much darker than his, I stitched up the body of a dead man.

CAPTAIN. A dead man! What do you mean?

BABA. Ah. You want me to speak, but you shall know no more.

The Captain pulls out a gold coin, and puts it into Baba Mustapha's hand.

CAPTAIN. I merely ask you to do me one small favour. Show me the dead man's house.

BABA. Even if I wanted to, I couldn't. I was blindfold. I didn't see a thing.

CAPTAIN. Come on, let me blindfold you again. We'll see if you can retrace your steps.

The Captain gives Baba Mustapha a second coin.

Baba Mustapha holds the two pieces of gold in his hand, deliberating, then pockets them.

CAPTAIN. To the great joy of the captain of the forty thieves ...

BABA. . . . he stood up and led the Captain to the spot where Marjanah had bound his eyes.

The Captain blindfolds Baba Mustapha. Baba leads off, retracing his steps.

Baba Mustapha led the thief to Kasim's house, where Ali Baba now lived.

CAPTAIN. The Captain sent the old man on his way and raced back to the forest where he ordered the thieves to buy twenty mules and forty large leather jars, one full of oil and the others completely empty. He made each man, armed with his spiky dagger, climb inside a jar and loaded two jars on each mule.

The thieves climb inside jars by wrapping themselves in their capes which are now lined with leather.

Then they set off for town and arrived as twilight shadows fell on Ali Baba's doorstep . . .

Captain puts on his oil merchant disguise.

ALI BABA. . . . where the owner was taking in some fresh evening air . . .

SON. . . . with his son . . .

CAPTAIN. Sir, my name is Kawaja Husain. I have brought some oil from a faraway place, to sell at market tomorrow. Would it be possible to spend the night under your roof?

ALI BABA. Ali Baba didn't recognise The Captain through his disguise.

Welcome!

He opens the gates to allow the mules into the yard.

CAPTAIN. Kawaja Husain, or rather the captain of the forty thieves, unloaded the jars. He went from jar to jar saying:

Have your daggers at the ready. When the time is right I shall return and give the signal.

After this, he went back into the house, to join Ali Baba for supper.

MARJANAH. Marjanah set about preparing a rich, tasty meal. While she was cooking, the oil lamp in the kitchen went out and there were no candles or oil to be found in the house. So, she picked up the oil pot and went into the yard to borrow some from one of the forty jars. When she drew close to the first jar . . .

SHAHRAZAD (*inside one of the jars*). . . . the thief inside whispered: Is it time yet?

MARJANAH. Not yet. But soon.

Jar by jar she went round quietly, giving the same answer, until she came to the jar filled with oil.

This way, Marjanah learned that there were forty vengeful thieves in the house and that this so-called oil merchant was their captain.

The second she lit the lamp she took the biggest pan in the house and filled it to the brim with thick, gloopy oil. She rushed to the kitchen and set it onto a crackling fire. As soon as it bubbled and spat, she picked it up and took it out.

Marjanah kills the thieves in their jars.

When she had done this, she went to serve the food and wine.

Captain, Ali Baba and Son eat and drink..

CAPTAIN. Just then the Captain hatched a bloodthirsty scheme.

There's no need to call my men, he thought.

I will get them both drunk, so they fall asleep. Then, I shall slice my enemy in two like a ripe watermelon.

MARJANAH. However, Marjanah had spotted the Captain of the Forty Thieves' knife through his clothes and knew what he was up to.

She put on her dancer's veil.

Marjanah bows deeply.

ALI BABA. Come in Marjanah. Kawaja Husain will tell us what he thinks of your performance.

Marjanah pulls out the dagger and performs a hugely energetic, mesmerising, sensual, sometimes violent dance in which she alternates between thrusting the dagger outwards as if to stab someone and sometimes inwards as if to stab herself in the chest. Eventually Marjanah kills the Captain.

ALI BABA. Wretched woman, what have you done? You've ruined us all.

MARJANAH. I did this to save you, not ruin you.

Look closely and you shall recognise the captain of the forty thieves.

ALI BABA. I owe my life to you. I give you your freedom from this moment and if he will agree, my son's hand in marriage.

SON. Far from refusing, his son was delighted . . .

SON *and* MARJANAH. . . . and a few days later . . .

SON. . . . with a sacred blessing . . .

MARJANAH. . . . and an extravagant feast,

SON *and* MARJANAH. . . . they were married!

Short wedding tableau that echoes Shahrayar and Shahrazad, except this time full of joy and light. Just as the married couple kiss, Shahrayar interrupts and the characters freeze.

Threat

The King's room. Dawn.

Sound of a sword being sharpened.

SHAHRAYAR. So you think he was happy? This son of Ali Baba?

SHAHRAZAD. So the story goes.

SHAHRAYAR. He marries a crafty cunning woman and lives in a fine house. He is sure be tricked and lied to and crushed by this scheming slavegirl.

SHAHRAZAD. My lord, the story says otherwise.

SHAHRAZAD. Your story is written by a liar. Executioner!

DINARZAD. I know you have many other tales, sister. Perhaps you could tell us one tonight.

SHAHRAYAR. I have no more time to listen to your sister's prattling. Executioner!

SHAHRAZAD. What a shame, for tonight I would have told you the intriguing hilarious tale of . . .

The Executioner grabs her and leads her out.

SHAHRAYAR. One word. Before you go.

They stop.

What was the name of the story you were going to tell me?

SHAHRAZAD. The Story of The Little Beggar.

SHAHRAYAR. What sort of story is it?

SHAHRAZAD. One to put a smile on a King's face.

SHAHRAYAR. Laughter died with my first wife.

SHAHRAZAD. The King in this story finds laughter where he least expects it.

Pause.

SHAHRAYAR. I have a mind to hear it. You shall tell me tonight. Tomorrow, Vizier.

Vizier signals to the Headsman to let Shahrazad go. Shahrazad, Dinarzad and Vizier share a moment of relief. Exit Vizier and Headsman.

SHAHRAZAD. The day melted into night.

DINARZAD. And an hour before dawn, Dinarzad said:

Sister, if you are not too sleepy, tell us another strange and wonderful story.

SHAHRAZAD. May I tell my story, my Lord?

SHAHRAYAR. You may.

SHAHRAZAD. Very well.

Listen . . .

The Story of the Little Beggar

A raised area with steps is required for this story. This might be a ladder or a moveable platform.

SHAHRAZAD. Once there lived a tailor, with a pretty and faithful wife . . .

TAILOR. . . . One day while taking a walk . . .

TAILOR'S WIFE. . . . they bumped into a jolly little beggar.

He is smartly dressed with a scarf and a tall green hat, improvising a slapstick death routine with singing and tambourine. The tailor and wife laugh and clap.

TAILOR. When they got close they could smell wine on his breath and realised that he was roaring drunk.

He puts his tambourine under his arm and claps his hands in time with his song:

BEGGAR. If you fancy cheering up
Feed my belly and fill my cup!

TAILOR'S WIFE. The tailor and his wife took so strongly to the Little Beggar that they asked him to come home with them to eat.

TAILOR *and* TAILOR'S WIFE. They all sat down to a delicious meal of bread and fish.

TAILOR. They ate and drank till they had finished everything . . .

TAILOR'S WIFE. . . . except for one large fish.

TAILOR. I know. I bet you can't swallow this whole.

He tries to swallow it.

TAILOR'S WIFE. But a sharp piece of fishbone got stuck in his throat.

He starts choking and falls to the floor. The tailor and wife, clap and laugh thinking it is an act, till his body is still.

They prod him. They check him. He is stone dead.

Silence.

TAILOR'S WIFE. Don't just sit there. Do something.

TAILOR. What?

TAILOR'S WIFE. Pick him up, wrap him in a sheet, and follow me.

TAILOR. The tailor did as his wife said . . .

TAILOR'S WIFE. . . . . till they arrived at the house of a doctor.

They go up some stairs.

The wife knocks at the door.

MAID. A maid answered.

Tailor's wife hands the maid a coin.

TAILOR'S WIFE. Miss, please give this to your master. Ask him to come to see my child who is dangerously ill.

The maid goes to fetch the doctor.

They rest the body in the doorway and run off.

MAID. Master, there is a sick child with its parents downstairs. They gave me a quarter piece of gold for you.

DOCTOR. Light, light, quickly, girl, quickly.

TAILOR'S WIFE. Put down the beggar and run.

He rushes through in the dark and accidentally kicks the corpse down the stairs.

The maid comes with a candle.

The doctor takes an arm and feels the pulse. Nothing.

DOCTOR. I am finished. I have killed the patient I was supposed to cure. How will I get this body out of my house?

So he carried the little beggar upstairs to his wife.

WIFE. You're neither use nor ornament! What are you sitting there for with a face like a bottle of warts? If the day breaks and he is still here, they will hang us as murderers. I know. You must drop him down the chimney of our next-door neighbour, the King's Steward. The cats and dogs often eat his larder clean of meat and butter. Perhaps they will eat up this body.

The doctor and his wife take the little beggar up on the roof and drop him down the chimney. The little beggar lands on his feet. He stands, still wrapped in his blanket, bolt upright, leaning against a wall.

STEWARD. Just then, the King's Steward came home.

He opens the door, with a candle in his hand and sees the body.

What's this? A burglar? So it's not the cats and dogs who have been eating my meat and butter, it's a man.

He picks up a stick and cracks it over the little beggar. The little beggar falls. He gives him another blow on the back. He prods him. And again. Lifts up his eyelids and realises he is dead.

What have I done? Curses on my meat and butter!

He puts the Beggar on his back.

So he carried the Little Beggar to the marketplace and leaned him up against a shop.

Again, he stands upright.

MERCHANT. At that moment, a wealthy merchant, the King's Broker, staggered by in a drunken stupor.

He stands against the wall next to but without noticing the Little Beggar and relieves himself. In his drunkenness, he sways into the corpse, which falls onto the Merchant's back with arms round his neck.

MERCHANT. Thief! Thief! Watchman! Help me!

The Merchant throws the Little Beggar to the floor with a sharp blow and begins pummelling and choking him.

WATCHMAN (*enters*) What is it?

MERCHANT. Ah Watchman, this man tried to rob me.

Watchman checks the Little Beggar to see if he is breathing and listens to his chest.

WATCHMAN. You've killed him. You're coming with me.

He grabs the Merchant and ties him up.

WATCHMAN. The Watchman took him to the Chief of
Police . . .

CHIEF. . . . who threw him in a cell and, next morning, went
to tell the King . . .

KING. . . . who ordered the merchant to be hanged.

CHIEF. And the Chief went to the Hangman . . .

HANGMAN. . . . who set up a gallows and announced the
execution.

*Public execution. The Merchant stands on a box. The
Hangman places noose around his neck. Drum roll.*

STEWARD (*from the audience*). Stop. This man is not guilty.
I am to blame for his death.

CHIEF. What did you say?

STEWARD. I am to blame for his death.

And the steward told how he hit the Little Beggar with a
stick.

Hang me instead.

CHIEF. Release the merchant. Hang this man instead.

*The Hangman takes the noose off the Merchant who steps
down from the box. The Steward stands on the box. The
Hangman places noose around his neck. Drum roll.*

DOCTOR (*from the audience*). Stop. This man is innocent.
The guilt lies at my door.

And the doctor told how he had kicked the Little Beggar
down the stairs. Hang me instead.

CHIEF. Release the merchant and hang the doctor.

*The Hangman takes the noose off the Merchant who steps
down from the box. The Doctor stands on the box. The
Hangman places noose around his neck. Drum roll.*

TAILOR (*from the audience*) Stop. This man didn't kill the Little Beggar. No one killed him but me.

And the merchant told how he had choked the Little Beggar with a fishbone and left the body at the Doctor's house.

Hang me instead.

CHIEF. I've never heard the like. Release the doctor and hang the tailor.

The Hangman starts to take the noose off the Doctor who steps down from the box.

DOCTOR. But –

CHIEF. Any more interruptions and I'll hang the lot of you.

DOCTOR. But . . .

CHIEF. WHAT IS IT?

DOCTOR. This body is still breathing.

All turn to look at the Little Beggar's body There is a strange choking sound. The doctor opens his bag and takes out a giant pair of tweezers, opens the Little Beggar's mouth and puts them down his throat pulling out a huge fishbone.

BEGGAR (*huge sneeze. Stands bolt upright*).

If you fancy cheering up
Feed my belly and fill my cup!

TAILOR. And word reached the King.

KING. I've never heard a more extraordinary story in my life.

And the King was so delighted that he awarded robes of honour . . .

TAILOR. . . . to the tailor . . .

Tailor steps forward to receive his robe.

DOCTOR. . . . doctor . . .

Doctor steps forward to receive his robe.

STEWARD. . . . steward . . .

Steward steps forward to receive his robe.

MERCHANT. . . . and merchant . . .

Tailor steps forward to receive his robe

KING. . . . and sent them on their way thanking them for entertaining him with such an excellent story.

BEGGAR. And the Little Beggar was appointed the King's jester . . .

SHAHRAZAD. . . . and made the king chuckle for the rest of his days.

King starts smiling, giggles then a loud laugh cracks through him.

Warning

The King's room. Dawn.

Sound of a sword being sharpened.

SHAHRAYAR. This laughing king is a fool like I once was. Before I learned the truth about women. Laughter should be a stranger to a king's heart.

Enter Vizier.

VIZIER. What shall I tell the executioner, my lord?

DINARZAD. I would love to hear another of your wonderful stories tonight.

SHAHRAZAD. I will tell you one. An extraordinary tale of adventure and survival against all odds. If the King spares my life.

SHAHRAYAR. Do you take me for a fool, woman?

SHAHRAZAD. I know you to be the wisest of men, my lord.

SHAHRAYAR. Then why do you think you can trick me?

SHAHRAZAD. Trick you, your majesty?

SHAHRAYAR. Trying to tempt me with your senseless stories!

SHAHRAZAD. If you feel you are being tricked, Good King, I shall never breathe a word of a story again.

SHAHRAYAR. I will be the one to decide that.

SHAHRAZAD. Yes, my lord.

SHAHRAYAR. I hear your stories as and when I choose. And when I no longer choose, you will die like the others.

SHAHRAZAD. As your majesty pleases.

SHAHRAYAR. Vizier, you may go.

Shahrazad, Dinarzad and Vizier share a moment of relief.

SHAHRAZAD. The day melted into night.

DINARZAD. And an hour before dawn, Dinarzad said:

Sister, if you are not too sleepy, tell us another strange and wonderful story.

SHAHRAZAD. May I, my Lord?

SHAHRAYAR. Go on.

SHAHRAZAD. Very well.

Listen . . .

The Story of Es-Sindibad the Sailor

Es-Sindibad the Sailor uses a puppet of his younger self to act out much of his story. The rest of the images are created by the company using masks, models and puppets.

SHAHRAZAD. Once, in the city of Baghdad, there lived a poor man who earned his living by carrying loads on his head. He was called Es-Sindibad the Porter.

One day, as he was staggering under a heavy load in the sweltering heat of the summer sun, he stopped to rest.

He found himself in a shaded spot by a fine merchant's house. A cool and fragrant breeze blew through the doorway, and from within floated the sweet strains of a kamanja.

PORTER (*sings*). Heavy my burden and desperate my state,
Forsaken by fortune, cursed by fate.
Others are wealthy and charmed is their life.
Shielded from worry, sheltered from strife.

Many men toil in the sun to get paid.
Whilst others they rest and recline in the shade.

He finishes the song and places his load on his head.

PORTER. Just as he was about to go on his way . . .

PAGE. . . . a smartly dressed page appeared.

The page takes him by the hand.

PAGE. Please come in. My master would like to speak with you.

PORTER. The porter politely declined . . .

PAGE. . . . but the page would not be deterred.

PORTER. So, Es-Sindibad left his load at the door and followed the page into the house.

He was led into a magnificent and spacious hall, as splendid as the palace of a king. At one end sat a distinguished old man whose beard was touched with silver.

Sindibad the porter kisses the ground before his host.

SAILOR. You are welcome, my friend. May this day bring you joy. What is your name and what do you do?

PORTER. My name is Es-Sindibad. By trade a porter.

SAILOR. How strange! For my name is also Es-Sindibad. Es-Sindibad the Sailor. I heard your song.

PORTER. Please don't reproach me, sir. Poverty and hardship teach a man bad manners.

SAILOR. Do not be ashamed, for you have become a brother to me. I found your song delightful.

Porter, I should like to tell you the story of how I came to own this fine house. For my wealth was not won without huge effort, much pain and grave, grave danger.

He indicates for the porter to sit. The porter sits.

Know this. My father was the owner of untold wealth and property. He died when I was a little boy and left it all to me. When I was a young man, (*Sailor produces a puppet of his younger self, which he uses to act out the rest of the story.*) I ate and drank freely, wore fine clothes and frittered my days away chatting and joking with friends, as if my wealth would last forever. By the time I came to my senses, I found that my money was spent and I was ruined.

Fear swallowed my heart. How on earth was I going to survive? In a trice, the answer came to me. I would see the world and not come back to Baghdad until I had made my fortune. So, I sold all my possessions, put my best foot forward and boarded a ship with a group of merchants bound for the golden city of El-Basrah.

One of the company brings on the model of the ship which circles Es-Sindibad as in a memory or dream.

We passed from island to island, from sea to sea, from country to country and bought and sold and bargained until we came to a beautiful island. It was rich with leafy trees, mellow fruits, fragrant flowers, singing birds and crystal water. But there was not a soul to be seen.

I sat in the shade by a soothing stream. I ate my food and sipped on some wine. The air was heavy with the musk of wild flowers and before long I had drifted into a deep, deep sleep.

I cannot tell how long I slept, but when I awoke, the other passengers had gone. The ship had sailed with everyone on board, and no one remembered me.

Broken with terror and despair I collapsed on the sand. I wailed. I beat my chest. I cursed myself a thousand times

for leaving Baghdad. For I was all alone without a crumb to
eat or a thing to my name. I thought I was going mad.

*The puppet of Es-Sindibad climbs a tree and gazes from left
to right.*

I scrambled up a tree. I gazed from left to right.

All I could see was sky and water and trees and birds and
islands and sand. But when I scanned the island more
closely, I noticed, to my surprise, a strange white object
looming in the distance.

Puppet approaches a huge white egg.

I walked round it. I could find no door. Because the surface
was smooth and sleek, I couldn't climb up.

He walks round, counting the circumference pace by pace.

I stood there puzzling over how to get inside, when
suddenly the sky turned black.

*A gigantic bird played by one of the company, hovers over
the puppet.*

In a flash I was reminded of a story I had once heard from
an adventurer. In a faraway island there lives a bird of
monstrous size called a Rukh, which feeds its young on
elephants. Instantly, I realised that this dome was none other
than a Rukh's egg.

*The bird lands on the egg and falls asleep. Puppet creeps
close and stands by one of its legs.*

When The Rukh was fast asleep, I sprung into action.

Puppet uses his turban to tie himself to the bird's foot.

Praise be to Allah. This bird will carry me out of here. To
civilisation.

*Daybreak; the bird wakes up, screeches loudly and flies,
carrying the puppet up to the sky, soaring higher and
higher. It slowly swoops into land. When it does, the puppet
escapes, and the bird flies away.*

I found myself at the base of a valley as deep as dread, surrounded by mountains so high, they stabbed the clouds like spears. Why didn't I stay on the island? I am a fool, an idiot, a moron.

I walked around the valley and was staggered to find that the ground was covered with priceless diamonds, The entire valley blazed in glorious light. To my horror, here and there amongst the shimmering stones, were coils of deadly snakes, each large enough to swallow a camel. (*The company play snakes using glove puppets.*) They were slithering back to their darkened dens. For, in daylight, they hid in fear of being carried away by rukhs and eagles and eaten.

Consumed by terror and weak with hunger, I roamed the valley all day, searching for somewhere safe to spend the night.

Suddenly, something fell out of the sky and landed smack bang in front of me with a loud thud. It was a joint of lamb!

I was baffled, for there was not a soul in sight. Who or what could have thrown this meat? Quick as a wink, it came to me. I recalled a story I had once heard from travellers who had visited the valley of the diamonds. It is a place too dangerous to enter. But some crafty merchants have hit upon a wily scheme to gather jewels from the valley floor. At dawn, they would take a sheep, kill it, cut it up, and throw the pieces from the top of the mountain into the valley. The meat is fresh and moist and the diamonds stick to it. At midday, they wait until Eagles swoop down, pick up the meat and lift it away in their talons to their nests at the top of the mountain. With a mighty din, the merchants would rush at the birds. This would scare the eagles away, leaving the meat in the nest and the diamonds for the merchants.

Till that moment I truly believed I would never leave this valley alive. But at a stroke, I started to see a way out.

Not wishing to waste the riches at my feet, I gathered as many of the biggest diamonds I could find. I stuffed my pockets, my clothes, even my shoes to bursting.

Es-Sindibad grabs the meat and lies underneath it.

An eagle enters, Es-Sindibad waves at it. It swoops down, grabs the meat between its talons and soars up into the air, with Es-Sindibad clinging on for dear life. The eagle lands in its nest. Enter another puppet, The Merchant, shouting and clattering wood. The eagle flies away in fear and Es-Sindibad frees himself from the meat and stands by its side. The merchant who had been shouting comes to inspect the slaughtered sheep. He doesn't see Es-Sindibad.

MERCHANT. No diamonds? What a catastrophe! However could that have happened?

ES-SINDIBAD. Hello, friend.

MERCHANT. Who are you? What the devil are you doing here?

ES-SINDIBAD. Do not be alarmed, sir. I am an honest man, a sailor by profession. Please accept some of these diamonds, which I myself gathered in the valley below.

He gives the merchant some diamonds.

ES-SINDIBAD. These will bring you all the riches you could wish for.

MERCHANT. A thousand thanks, good man.

ES-SINDIBAD. When the other merchants heard me talking to their friend they trooped over.

Three other merchant puppets come over.

They greeted and congratulated me on my remarkable escape and took me with them. I told them my story.

MERCHANT 2. Allah has granted you a charmed life. For no one has set foot in the valley and come out alive.

MERCHANT 3. Allah be praised.

They gave me food and drink and I slept soundly for many hours.

At daybreak, we set off on our journey over the great mountains together. On the way, I exchanged some of my

diamonds for rich merchandise and supplies including a
magic lantern and a flying carpet.

We traded from port to port and island to island till finally
we reached Baghdad, the City of Peace.

SHAHRAZAD. When Es-Sindibad had finished telling his
story, he gave Es-Sindibad the Porter a hundred pieces of
gold.

The porter returned many times to the house of his
illustrious friend, to hear more of his adventures, and the
two lived in friendship for the rest of their lives.

Dawn

The King's bedroom. Dawn.

Sound of a sword being sharpened.

SHAHRAYAR. This sailor seems to survive every danger he
faces. Is no challenge too great for him?

SHAHRAZAD. Allah has blessed him with the gift of cunning,
your majesty.

Enter Vizier expectantly.

SHAHRAYAR. Word has reached me, Shahrazad, that the
people are praising your name for saving their daughters
over these last few months. You are quite a heroine. Are you
proud of yourself?

SHAHRAZAD. If I please the people, then I please the king,
as king and people are one.

SHAHRAYAR. I hope for the people's sake that the well of
your stories does not dry up.

SHAHRAZAD. Yes, my lord.

SHAHRAYAR. For I have given my word.

SHAHRAZAD. And a king's word is sacred.

SHAHRAYAR. Well aren't you afraid?

SHAHRAZAD. I may be afraid of dying. But not of death. I have been blessed with a life filled with joy. I would rather have short joyful life than a long life in the darkness. Life without joy is a living death.

Pause.

Shahrayar nods to Vizier.

Shahrazad, Dinarzad and Vizier share a moment of relief.

Vizier goes.

SHAHRAZAD. Listen . . .

How Abu Hassan Broke Wind

SHAHRAZAD. It is said that in the city of Kaukaban in Yemen there was a man who was the wealthiest of merchants called Abu Hassan. His wife had died when she was very young and his friends were always pressing him to marry again.

ABU. So, weary of being nagged, Abu Hassan approached an old woman . . .

MARRIAGE BROKER. . . . a marriage-broker . . .

WIFE. . . . who found him a wife with eyes as dark as a desert night and a face as fresh as the dawn.

ABU. He arranged a sumptuous wedding banquet and invited . . .

UNCLE. . . . uncles . . .

AUNT. . . . and aunts . . .

PREACHER. . . . preachers and fakirs . . .

FRIEND. . . . friends . . .

FOE. . . . and foes . . .

Shahrayar now joins the world of the stories as a guest.

GREAT AND GOOD. . . . and the great and the good from all around.

ALL. The whole house was thrown open for feasting.

UNCLE. There was rice . . .

AUNT. . . . of five colours . . .

PREACHER. . . . sherbets of many more . . .

FRIEND. . . . goats stuffed with walnuts . . .

FOE. . . . and almonds and pistachios . . .

GREAT AND GOOD. . . . and a whole roast camel.

ALL. So they ate and drank and made merry . . .

BRIDE. . . . and the bride was displayed, as is the custom, in her seven dresses to the women . . .

WOMEN. . . . who couldn't take their eyes off her.

ABU HASSAN. At last, the bridegroom was summoned to go up to his wife . . .

WIFE. . . . who sat on a golden throne . . .

ABU HASSAN. . . . and he rose with stately dignity from the sofa. When all of a sudden he let fly a huge and deafening fart.

A deafening fart is heard.

AUNT. Immediately each guest turned to his neighbour . . .

FAKIR. . . . and busied himself in pressing conversation . . .

UNCLE. . . . as if his life depended on it. . . .

ABU HASSAN. But a fire of shame was lit in Abu Hassan's heart, so he excused himself and instead of going to his wife, went down to the stables, saddled his horse and rode off weeping bitter tears through the blackness of the night.

In time he reached Lahej where he boarded a ship bound for India where he remained for ten long years. When finally he returned, his eyes burned with tears when he saw his old house and he said to himself:

I hope no one recognises me. I shall wander round the
outskirts and listen to the people's gossip. Allah grant no
one remembers my shameful deed.

He trudged around for seven days and seven nights, until he
found himself sitting on the doorstep of a hut. From inside,
he heard the voice of a young girl;

GIRL. Mother, tell me what day I was born. One of my friends
wants to tell my fortune.

MOTHER. You were born on the very night that Abu Hassan
did his famous fart.

Abu Hassan jumps up and runs away.

SHAHRAZAD. And he didn't stop travelling till he arrived
back in India, where he remained for the rest of his days.

Awakening

The King's room. Dawn.

*Shahrayar has turned his back on Shahrazad. Shahrayar is
smiling.*

SHAHRAZAD. Did you enjoy the story, my lord?

*Shahrayar giggles, laughs, then a huge bellyaching laugh
rips out of him. Dinarzad and Shahrazad start laughing too.*

Enter Vizier.

He stares at the King, bemused.

Lights fade to a solo spot on the laughing King.

Blackout.

Interval.

ACT TWO

The Story of the Wife Who Wouldn't Eat

Sidi 1 tells this story to Haroun and Sidi 2 acts it out in flashback. They are identifiable as the same person by distinctive items of the same clothing.

SHAHRAZAD. The great Caliph Haroun Al-Rashid often went out into the city of Baghdad in disguise, to find out more about the lives of his people. Once, on such a trip, he saw a huge crowd of spectators in the market square.

Enter horse (Amina) and Sidi 2 who ride round the stage furiously.

They were watching a handsome young man ride a horse at full speed. He was whipping her so harshly that she was wrapped in ribbons of blood.

HAROUN. The caliph was shocked by the young man's cruelty, and he asked his loyal Vizier to summon the young man to the palace. The following day, the young man came and kissed the ground before Haroun Al-Rashid. The Caliph asked his name and he replied:

SIDI 1. Sidi Nu'uman.

HAROUN. I have seen horses trained all my life, Sidi Nu'uman, but never, I am glad to say, in such a cruel, heartless way as you did yesterday. The spectators were horrified and so was I. You do not seem such a fearsome man, yet I am told, you do the same brutal thing every day. I would like to know the cause and have called you here today to give me a full and thorough explanation.

SIDI 1. I dare say that the way I treat my horse may seem cruel and heartless. When you hear the reasons why, you will see that I am more worthy of pity than blame.

HAROUN. Tell me your story.

SIDI 1. As is our country's custom, I married having never seen or met my wife. When she took off her veil after our wedding, I was pleased. I had feared she might be old, ugly and wrinkled but she seemed charming.

We see Sidi 2 unveil Amina. She lays out two plates of rice.

The day after our wedding, I sat down to lunch and began to eat my rice, as usual, heartily, with a spoon,

As he speaks we see this.

My wife, however, pushed her spoon aside.

Amina pulls a little case out of her pocket. She opens it and takes out a small pair of tweezers. She uses these to pick up the rice and nibble at it, grain by grain.

Young Sidi watches her, agog. She eats politely, as if this was the proper thing to do.

SIDI 1. Surprised at this, I said to her . . .

SIDI 2. . . . Amina . . .

SIDI 1. . . . for that was her name . . .

SIDI 2. . . . Is it a family tradition of yours to eat your rice so daintily or do you have a small appetite?

Amina carries on eating with the tweezers.

If you are doing it to save money, then don't worry, I promise we could afford ten thousand plates of rice and still have money to spare.

SIDI 1. My politeness and patience fell on deaf ears.

She continues to eat slowly, grain by grain.

The following night, at supper, she did exactly the same thing. And the next night and the next.

I knew it was impossible for anyone to live on so little food. I decided to get to the bottom of this mystery.

One night when Amina thought me fast asleep,

Sidi 2 acts out the following.

. . . she slithered softly out of bed. I pretended to keep my eyes shut but secretly was watching her like a hungry hawk.

She dresses and tiptoes out of the room.

The moment she turned her back, I got up and put on my robe.

I ran down to the front door and followed her by the eerie light of the moon, to a nearby graveyard. I hid behind the wall and peeked over when I saw Amina with a ghoul.

Amina dances a monstrous dance with the ghoul.

I watched with horror as they dug up a body that had been buried that day, cut the flesh into several pieces and ate it up, slavering and slobbering over their sickening feast in a way that makes me shudder to think about.

As they were filling up the grave with earth, I hurried home.

Sidi 2 goes to bed. As Amina approaches, he feigns sleep. She gets into bed beside him. Amina belches.

The next day, at dinner, she started to eat in her usual way.

They eat together as before, Amina again eats with tweezers.

SIDI 2. Amina, won't you eat some more?

Amina shakes her head.

SIDI 2. Are you sure?

Amina shakes her head.

SIDI 2. Amina, dearest, does the food at my table not taste better than dead flesh?

SIDI 1. It was then that I learned that Amina was an evil sorceress.

Amina dips her hand into a basin of water and throws it into Sidi 2's face with the words.

AMINA.
By the power of water drawn from a bog
Nosy wretch turn into a dog!

Sidi 2 becomes a dog and yaps pathetically at Amina. She grabs a stick and chases him with it, beating him. He outruns her. She grabs his tail meanly. He whimpers and nips her. He runs off barking and howling.

SIDI 1. I ran out of the house and into the street. Before long, all the local stray dogs were chasing after me.

Chase sequence. Whole company as dogs chasing Sidi Nu'uman through the audience and biting him where possible.

I took refuge in the doorway of a baker's who was cheerful and kind.

BAKER. Hello Dog.

The baker throws Sidi 2 a piece of bread. He licks the baker's face and wags his tail to show his appreciation. The baker laughs. Sidi then eats the piece of bread.

SIDI 1. The baker let me stay in the shop and gave me a place to sleep.

If I was out of sight, he would call . . .

BAKER. . . . Chance! . . .

SIDI 1. . . . which was the name he gave me . . .

BAKER. . . . Chance!!

Sidi 2 comes scooting in and jumps and flies up to his master, running round and round, being a playful obedient dog.

SIDI 1. One day, a woman came into the shop to buy some bread. She paid with several coins, one of which was false, and completely worthless. My master noticed the bad coin and gave it back asking for another.

CUSTOMER 1. There is nothing wrong with this coin.

BAKER. Yes there is..

CUSTOMER. No there isn't.

BAKER. This coin is so obviously fake. Even my dog could pick it out.

CUSTOMER 1. Go on then. Ask him.

BAKER. Very well. Chance! Chance!

The dog approaches.

BAKER. Look at these coins, Chance. Tell me which one is false.

Sidi 2 examines and sniffs each coin and then sets his paw on the bad one, separates it from the rest, and stares his master in the face, to await approval.

SIDI 1. The baker was staggered. The woman changed the bad coin for a good one and left, stunned into silence. She was sure to tell everyone she met about me. Soon I became a local celebrity.

Not long after this, another woman came to buy some bread.

Customer 2 throws down six coins on the counter. Sidi 2 places his paw on one of the coins and looks up at the woman.

CUSTOMER 2. Yes, you are quite right; that is the bad one.

The woman beckons for Sidi 2 to come with her. He hesitates for a moment and then follows her out of the shop.

Several streets away, she stopped at a house and beckoned me in.

CUSTOMER 2. You won't regret following me.

He follows her in.

SIDI 1. When I went in I saw a beautiful young lady with a smile as sweet as hope.

CUSTOMER 2. Daughter, I have brought you the famous baker's dog. Remember when I first heard about him, I had a hunch he was a man changed into a dog. Now tell me, daughter, am I mistaken in my suspicion?

SORCERESS. No, mother, you are not. As I shall prove.

Sorceress dips her hand into a basin of water and throws it into Sidi 2's face with the words.

If you were cursed by evil plan
By the power of water change back to a man!

Sidi 2 returns to his old self.

SIDI 2. My debt to you is greater than I could ever repay.

SIDI 1. After I had told her who I was, I gave an account of my marriage to Amina, her curious eating, the horrible sight I saw in the graveyard and how I came to be changed into a dog.

SORCERESS. I know Amina of old. She must be punished once and for all. Take this bottle. Go home immediately, and hide in your bedroom. As soon as Amina comes in throw this potion at her, pronouncing clearly and boldly;

By the power of potion brewed over time
Receive the punishment for your crime!

SIDI 2. By the power of potion brewed over time . . .

SIDI 2 *and* SORCERESS.
. . . Receive the punishment for your crime.

SORCERESS. I will tell you no more. You shall see the result.

Sidi 2 waits in his bedroom.. Amina enters and meets him face to face; she screams and turns, about to run to the door. He throws the potion over her. She freezes.

SIDI 2. By the power of potion brewed over time
Receive the punishment for your . . .
Receive the punishment for your . . .
Receive the punishment for your . . .

He looks for help from the audience.

AUDIENCE. crime!

SIDI 2. rhyme? etc . . .

AUDIENCE. crime!

SIDI 2.
By the power of potion brewed over time
Receive the punishment for your crime!

Amina transforms into a horse . Sidi 2 grabs her by the mane. He then rides her in a repeat of the first time we meet Sidi 1. Eventually, they leave the space.

Sidi 2 echoes first entrance of Sidi 1, riding and beating a horse.

SIDI 1. And I have ridden her and beaten her the same way every day, ever since. I hope your majesty will now agree that I have shown such a cruel and wicked woman more patience than she deserves.

HAROUN. Your story is quite remarkable, and the wickedness of your wife inexcusable. Therefore I can forgive some of your harshness towards her. However, being turned into an animal is surely punishment enough and you should not seek to hurt her any more. Revenge is like a deadly, climbing weed. If it lays its roots in your thoughts, it will not stop till it has strangled your heart and poisoned your soul. To be free, you must forgive.

SHAHRAZAD. The wise Caliph signified by the bowing of his head that Sidi Nu'uman was free to go. Sidi Nu'uman kissed the ground before him and retired.

Sidi strokes his horse and leads it away.

Promise

The King's room. Dawn.

Sound of a sword being sharpened.

Enter Vizier. He is now an old, old man.

He has just entered when the king signals for him to go. Without stopping he turns round and exits.

SHAHRAZAD. The day melted into night.

DINARZAD. And an hour before dawn . . .

SHAHRAYAR. King Shahrayar said:

What story do you have for me tonight?

SHAHRAZAD. A trifling tale, my lord.

SHAHRAYAR. One of many hundreds of trifling tales you
have told me already.

SHAHRAZAD. Eight hundred and seventeen, my lord.

SHAHRAYAR. Your wily woman's tongue has saved your
pretty head eight hundred and seventeen times. That's a
long time.

DINARZAD. Two years, two months, three weeks and four
days.

SHAHRAYAR. I can't seem to resist your stories my crafty
queen. Your trick is working. Well go on. Begin.

Shahrazad doesn't speak.

Speak.

Shahrazad remains silent.

SHAHRAYAR. I'm listening.

She is still silent.

I command you to tell me your story.

Shahrazad whispers to Dinarzad.

Well what is she saying?

DINARZAD. She says she dare not speak. In case she tries to
trick you with her cunning woman's words.

SHAHRAYAR. Tell her, I want to hear her story.

Dinarzad whispers to Shahrazad. Shahrazad whispers back.

DINARZAD. She says are you sure?

SHAHRAYAR. Tell her Yes!

Dinarzad whispers to her again. Shahrazad whispers back.

DINARZAD. Really sure?

SHAHRAYAR. Yes.

Dinarzad whispers to her.

SHAHRAYAR. ONE MORE WHISPER AND I'LL HAVE
    BOTH YOUR HEADS OFF!

SHAHRAZAD. Your majesty.

SHAHRAYAR. Wife.

SHAHRAZAD. What would you do if the well of my stories
    runs dry?

SHAHRAYAR. But that will never happen. (*Beat.*) Will it?

SHAHRAZAD. As there are so many grains of sand in the
    desert, there are only so many stories in my head. They are
    sure to run out one day. And on that day, I must die. For you
    have given your word.

SHAHRAYAR. I have.

SHAHRAZAD. And a king's word is sacred.

SHAHRAYAR. It is.

SHAHRAZAD. Shall I start then?

SHAHRAYAR. What?

SHAHRAZAD. My story.

SHAHRAYAR. Of course.

SHAHRAZAD. Very well.

    Listen . . .

The Story of the Envious Sisters

SHAHRAZAD. There was once a King in Persia called
    Khusrau Shah. One evening he went walking in the poorest
    area of the city, with his loyal Vizier, when he overheard
    laughter coming from the humblest house in the street. He
    approached, and peeking through a crack in the door, he
    saw three sisters sitting on a sofa having an after dinner
    chat. They were talking about wishes.

ELDEST SISTER. I wish I could marry the King's Baker. For then I would eat my belly full of bread. And royal bread is the finest in the city.

SECOND SISTER. I wish I could marry the King's cook. For then I would eat the most excellent meats. And meats are much tastier than bread.

YOUNGEST. I wish I could marry the King. For I would give him a beautiful baby prince, with hair like threads of silver and gold. When he cries, his tears will be pearls and when he smiles, his crimson lips will be fresh rose buds.

KING. The next day at the Palace, the King ordered his Vizier to bring the three sisters before him.

They kiss the floor before him.

They stand.

Last night you each made a wish. You wished to marry my baker. Your wish shall be granted today. You wished to marry my cook. Your wish shall be granted today. And you wished to marry me. Your wish shall be granted today.

YOUNGEST (*throws herself on floor*). Forgive me, your majesty, but my wish was only made by way of fun. I am not worthy of this honour.

The two elder sisters reluctantly copy.

ELDEST SISTERS. Forgive us, your majesty . . .

KING (*interrupting*). Silence! It shall be so. Everyone's wish shall be fulfilled.

THREE SISTERS. The weddings were celebrated that day . . .

TWO ELDEST. . . . but in very different style.

ELDEST. The eldest sister's marriage was celebrated in the pantry surrounded by sacks of flour.

SECOND. The second sister's marriage was celebrated in the kitchen surrounded by pots and pans.

YOUNGEST. The youngest sister was celebrated in the Royal Garden surrounded by jasmine and almond blossom.

ELDEST. Although their wishes had been granted . . .

SECOND. . . . the two elder sisters thought the difference between their weddings . . .

TWO ELDEST. . . . grossly unfair.

ELDEST. Their hearts were seized by a snake-like envy . . .

SECOND. . . . which not only strangled their own joy . . .

YOUNGEST. . . . but pierced their younger sister's happiness like a spiteful fang.

ELDEST. Well sister, what do you think of our grand little sister? Isn't she a fine one to be Queen?

SECOND. I must say, I have no idea what the King sees in her. To be so bewitched by the little madam. You are much more deserving. In fairness he should have chosen you.

ELDEST. Sister I wouldn't have batted an eyelid if the King had picked you, but that he should prefer that pert slut makes my blood boil. However I will be revenged. And you I think are of the same mind.

SECOND. From then on, whenever they visited the Queen, their sister . . .

ELDEST. . . . they would keep their vipers tongues hidden behind painted smiles.

YOUNGEST. And she would welcome them warmly and simply and treat them with the same love she always had.

Some months after their marriage, the queen found she was expecting a baby.

ELDEST. The sisters came to give their best wishes . . .

SECOND. . . . and offered to be by their sister's side when the baby was born . . .

TWO ELDEST. . . . as her midwives.

The actor playing Bahman makes the sound of a baby crying.

YOUNGEST. The Queen gave birth to a young prince as bright as morning.

ELDEST. But neither his sweetness . . .

SECOND. . . . nor his beauty . . .

TWO ELDEST. . . . could melt the icy hearts of the ruthless sisters.

ELDEST. They wrapped him in a coarse blanket, dropped him into a basket and floated him down a stream which ran past the queen's apartment.

SECOND. They then declared . . .

TWO ELDEST. . . . She gave birth to a dead dog.

They produce the dead dog.

KING. When the King was told, the world turned dark before his eyes and he ordered the Queen's head to be cut off.

VIZIER. But the kind Vizier stopped him, pleading that the queen could not be blamed for something that was not of her doing but nature's.

BAHMAN. Meanwhile, the basket, in which the little baby lay, floated downstream past the palace and through The King's gardens.

STEWARD. By chance the Steward of the King's Garden was waking past. When he saw the basket bobbing by, he fished it out and peered in. He was astonished to see a tiny baby sleeping inside.

The Steward took the baby to his house and showed him to his wife.

WIFE. The wife received the child with great joy, and took pleasure in looking after him as if he was her own.

YOUNGEST. A year later, the Queen had another baby prince.

The actor playing Bahman makes the sound of a baby crying.

TWO ELDEST. The wicked sisters were no kinder to him than the first.

FIRST. They put him in a basket and floated him down the stream . . .

SECOND. . . . announcing . . .

TWO ELDEST. She gave birth to a cat.

They show the dead cat.

KING. This time The King was determined to cut off the young Queen's head.

VIZIER. But again the Vizier stopped him pleading:

Let her live.

STEWARD. By happy chance, The Steward went walking by the stream again that day. So he took the second child to his wife and asked her to take as good care of it as the first.

WIFE. This suited her as well as it did her husband.

QUEEN. The third time the Queen became pregnant, she gave birth to a princess.

The actor playing Parizade makes the sound of a baby crying.

TWO ELDEST. The poor child suffered the same fate as her brothers.

SECOND. This time the sisters couldn't find an animal.

ELDEST. So they took a piece of wood and showed it, saying:

TWO ELDEST. She gave birth to a mole.

KING. The king could no longer contain himself.

This woman wants to fill my palace with monsters. She is a monster herself and I will rid the world of her.

VIZIER. Your majesty, laws are made to punish crimes. The three strange births of the Queen were not her fault. She is to be pitied not punished. Remove her from your eyes and heart, which is punishment enough, but let her live . . .

KING. Very well. But it shall be on one condition: that at least once a day, for the rest of her life, she curses the day she was born. Let a cell be built for her next to the mosque, with iron bars for windows and throw her in. Dress her in clothes that scratch her skin. And everyone that goes past shall spit in her face. See it done.

VIZIER. The Vizier knew better than to question the King in his rage. So he did as he was told . . .

ELDEST SISTERS. . . . to the great pleasure of the two envious sisters.

The Queen is thrown into a cell. Passers by spit.

STEWARD. That same day, The Steward was walking past the stream, and he took the third child to his wife and asked her to take as good care of it as the first two . . .

WIFE. . . . which she did most gladly.

TWO PRINCES. The two princes . . .

PRINCESS. . . . and the princess . . .

STEWARD. . . . were brought up by the Steward . . .

STEWARD'S WIFE. . . . and his wife . . .

STEWARD. . . . with all the tenderness of a true father . . .

WIFE. . . . and mother.

THREE CHILDREN. They were named after the kings and queens of Persia.

BAHMAN. They eldest prince was named Bahman. He was gentle and kind.

PERVIZ. The second was named Perviz. He was bold and headstrong.

PARIZADE. And the Princess was named Parizade.

BAHMAN. She was enchantingly beautiful . . .

PERVIZ. . . . and exceptionally clever.

STEWARD. As soon as the princes were old enough, the Steward provided them with the best teachers money could buy.

PARIZADE. Even though the princess was much younger, she would join in all their lessons and would often outshine them.

STEWARD. The Steward was delighted with his adopted children. So he set about building them a grand country house. He decked the rooms with priceless paintings and splendid furniture. He filled the garden with blazing flowers and fragrant shrubs. Then he stocked the nearby land with deer, so that the princes and princess could go hunting.

He lived in the house with the two princes Bahman and Perviz and princess Parizade for six months, when one day he shut his eyes and died.

BAHMAN. His wife had died some years before . . .

PERVIZ. . . . and his death was so sudden that he never told them the secret of their birth.

PARIZADE. The prince and the princess wept bitter tears of grief for the loving man they thought their father.

ALL THREE. But they were comforted by their beautiful house and lived there together in harmony.

WOMAN. One day, when the two princes were out hunting, an old religious woman arrived at the house. When she had said her prayers, she sat down with Parizade and chatted with her.

PARIZADE. Eventually Parizade asked her what she thought of the house?

WOMAN. Madam, it would be the King of houses but for three things . . .

PARIZADE. And what three things are they? I will do what I can to secure them.

WOMAN. The first of these things is the Talking Bird. This will draw a thousand coloured birds around it. The second is the singing tree. This will play a haunting harmony. The third is the Golden Water. This will form an everlasting fountain.

PARIZADE. I've never heard of such curious, wonderful things. Would you kindly tell me where they are?

WOMAN. Towards India, on the road that lies before your house. Whoever you send must travel twenty days. On the twentieth day they must ask the first person they meet where the talking bird, singing tree and golden fountain are. They shall be told.

If you find these three things, child, they will lead you to the truth about yourself.

PARIZADE. What do you mean?

WOMAN. And a fine lady shall be freed.

PARIZADE. I don't understand.

WOMAN. The road that lies before your house.

Exit Woman.

PARIZADE. Princess Parizade felt, in the pit of her stomach, that she had to have these things.

BAHMAN. When her brothers returned . . .

PERVIZ. . . . . they found their sister with her head weighed down . . .

BROTHERS. . . . . as if her thoughts were made of lead.

PARIZADE. So she told her brothers what the old woman had said.

BAHMAN. Tell me the place and the way there and I will leave tomorrow.

Early the next morning, Prince Bahman prepared his horse.

Parizade and Bahman embrace.

Bahman takes out a knife.

BAHMAN. Here sister, take this knife and every now and then, look at the blade. If it is clean, it is a sign I am alive. If it is stained with blood, then you must believe me dead, and pray for me.

On the twentieth day of his journey, he saw, by the side of the road a wise old man sitting under a tree.

BAHMAN. Good day, good father. I have come a long way in search of the talking bird, the singing tree and the golden water. Could you show me the way to them?

OLD MAN. Friendship forbids me to tell you.

BAHMAN. Why?

OLD MAN. A great number of fine gentlemen, as brave and courageous as you, have passed by here and asked me the very same question. Against my better judgement, I have told them the way and not one of them has ever come back. Son, if the gift of life means anything to you, go home now.

BAHMAN. I have a knife. If anyone attacks me I shall use it.

OLD MAN. What if your enemies are invisible?.

BAHMAN. Good father, no matter what you say, you will never persuade me to alter my course.

OLD MAN. Since I cannot force you to see sense, take this ball. When you are on horseback, throw it and follow it to the foot of a mountain where it will stop rolling. Leave your horse and start climbing the slope. You will see a large number of black stones and hear many threatening voices pressing you to turn round. They will try everything they can to stop you reaching the top of the mountain. But remember, whatever you hear behind you, however cruel, vicious or threatening: do not look back. For if you do, you will be turned into black stone like the other gentleman before you. If you manage to escape this danger and reach the top of the mountain you will see a cage. In that cage is the bird you seek. Ask him for the singing tree and golden water and he will show you. May the Heavens preserve you.

BAHMAN. Bahman thanked the wise old man, mounted his horse and threw the ball before him.

The ball rolls away. When it reaches the foot of the mountain, it stops.

The company become stones.

He looked up the mountain and saw the black stones, but had not gone four steps when the voices started:

The voices start quietly and escalate with every step he takes till they reach a murderous and deafening cacophony. Each actor repeats/improvises around the lines below. The same format is used for each attempt.

VOICE 1. You'll never make it to the top. A little weakling like you? (*Laughter etc.*)

VOICE 2. Turn around. There's a wolf behind you.

VOICE 3. That's it. Carry on. Just see what awaits you at the top of the slope! You are walking towards your death. etc.

VOICE 4. Go home. Your family are ill. They need your help. etc.

VOICE 5. You snivelling little wretch. You cockroach. You snake etc.

VOICE 6. I've got a surprise for you, sweet child, come and come and get your surprise.

VOICE 7. It's the devil's trick. Turn back. This is the voice of your father. Turn back!

Eventually Bahman's courage gives way and he turns. Instantly he is turned into stone.

PARIZADE. Just then Princess Parizade pulled the knife out of its sheath, as she did many times a day, to see if her brother was safe. Her heart froze to stone in her chest when she saw that the point was dripping with blood.

She throws down the knife.

Oh my dear brother I have been the cause of your death. I wish I had never met the old religious woman. Why did she tell me of the bird, the tree and the water?

PERVIZ. Our dear brother's death must not prevent us from pursuing our plan. Tomorrow I shall go myself.

PARIZADE. The princess begged him not to go . . .

PERVIZ. . . . but he was determined. Before he went, he left
her a necklace of a hundred pearls, telling her, from time to
time, to run her fingers along them.

If they move, I am alive. If they are fixed, then you know I
am dead.

PERVIZ. On the twentieth day of his journey, Prince Perviz
met the wise old man. Prince Perviz asked him, the same
way his brother had, where he could find the talking bird,
singing tree and golden water,

OLD MAN. And The Wise Old Man pleaded with Prince
Perviz to go home as he had to Prince Bahman.

PERVIZ. Good father, I have thought too long and hard about
this plan to give up now.

OLD MAN. As Prince Perviz could not be stopped, the Wise
Old Man handed him a ball, and told him to throw it and
follow it to the foot of the mountain. Then he gave Prince
Perviz the same warning he had given to Prince Bahman,
about the black stones and the threatening voices.

But remember, whatever you hear behind you, however
cruel, vicious or threatening; do not look back.

PERVIZ. Prince Perviz took leave of the wise man with a low
bow and threw the ball before him.

*The ball rolls away. When it reaches the foot of the
mountain, it stops.*

*Full company become stones, as before. Same escalation of
voices, but louder.*

*Prince Perviz gets very near the bird when the other voices
stop and a male stone just behind him says:*

STONE. My sword is drawn, weakling.

*When he hears this, Perviz draws his sword and turns
around. He is immediately turned into stone.*

PARIZADE. Just then, Princess Parizade was pulling on the
pearls of her necklace, as she did many times a day, when

all of a sudden, they stuck to the string. She knew then for certain that Prince Perviz was dead.

The next morning, she set out on the same road as her brothers. On the twentieth day, she met the wise old man.

PARIZADE. Parizade asked the old man where she could find the talking bird, singing tree and golden water,

OLD MAN. . . . And The Wise Old Man pleaded with her to turn round, as he had with her brothers.

PARIZADE. And give up my plan? I am sure I shall succeed.

OLD MAN. Because she would not heed his advice, the Wise Old Man gave her the ball and repeated the warning he had given to Prince Bahman and Prince Perviz about dreadful danger of the black stones and the threatening voices.

PARIZADE. From what you say, the only danger I face is getting to the cage without hearing the threatening voices. But that can be overcome quite simply.

WISE MAN. How?

PARIZADE. By stopping my ears with cotton.

WISE MAN. Of all the people who have asked me the way, I do not know of anyone who thought of that. If you must go, by all means try your trick. But remember, if you should hear anything on the mountain, however cruel, vicious or threatening: do not look back.

PARIZADE. After thanking him, she rode away and threw the ball before her.

The ball rolls away. When it reaches the foot of the mountain it stops.

Full company become stones, as before. Same escalation of volume, but even louder. She gets close to the bird who is a tiny glove puppet in a cage, operated by the Queen.

BIRD. Brave lady, if I have to be a slave I would rather be your slave than any in the world, since you have won me so courageously. From this moment, I swear a lifelong loyalty to you and promise to fulfil your every need.

PARIZADE. Thank you bird . . .

BIRD. I know who you really are and I can tell you. You are
not who think you are.

PARIZADE. What do you mean?

BIRD. You will find out in Allah's good time.

PARIZADE. Bird, I have been told that there is a singing tree
nearby. I want to know where it is.

BIRD. Turn around and you will see a wood behind you. You
will find the tree there.

She picks up the bird.

PARIZADE. The princess went into the wood. Her ears soon
led her to the tree.

Company become Singing Tree.

BIRD. Break off a branch and plant it in your garden. In a
short time it will grow into as fine a tree as you see here.

PARIZADE. Bird, I also want to find the golden water. Can
you show me to it?

The bird showed her the place that was very nearby and she
went and filled a silver flask she had brought.

Company become fountain.

PARIZADE. I have one more request. My brothers were turned
into black stones. I want you to free them.

BIRD. I have already done quite enough for today.

PARIZADE. I thought you said you were my slave and you
would fulfil my every need.

BIRD. Very well then. Look around and you will see a pitcher
of water.

PARIZADE. I see it.

BIRD. Pick it up, go down the hill and sprinkle some on every
black stone. You shall soon find your brothers.

Parizade picks up the pitcher and goes down the hill sprinkling water on every black stone. As soon as she does, it immediately turns into a man or a horse.

PARIZADE. Before long she found her brothers.

They embrace.

BAHMAN. She gave Prince Bahman the branch from the singing tree . . .

PERVIZ. . . . and Prince Perviz the golden water to carry . . .

ALL THREE. . . . and they set off for home.

PARIZADE. When the princess arrived, she placed the cage in the garden.

As soon as the bird starts to sing colourful birds swoop and glide around it.

BAHMAN. Then she planted the branch of the singing tree.

The tree sprouts up, each leaf singing a delightful tune and all joining together to play a harmonious concert.

PERVIZ. After that she poured the flask of golden water into a marble pool.

A fountain shoots up.

BAHMAN. Some days later, Prince Bahman . . .

PERVIZ. . . . and Prince Perviz . . .

TWO PRINCES. . . . went hunting in a nearby forest.

KING. As it happened, hunting in the same forest was the King.

They kiss the ground before the King.

KING. Who are you and where do you live?

BAHMAN. Sir, we are the sons of the late Steward of the King's Garden and we live in a house nearby.

KING. Perfect. I need somewhere to rest this evening. I should like to visit you.

PERVIZ. Your majesty, we would be honoured.

BAHMAN. Princes Bahman . . .

PERVIZ. . . . and Perviz . . .

BAHMAN. . . . pointed the king's courtiers to the house . . .

PARIZADE. . . . and hurried home to tell their sister.

PARIZADE. We must prepare a banquet for his majesty.

She goes to the bird.

PARIZADE. Bird, the King will be coming to visit tonight. What shall we give him to eat.

BIRD. Let your cooks prepare a dish of cucumbers stuffed with pearls.

PARIZADE. Cucumbers stuffed with pearls? That sounds disgusting. Besides where would I get enough pearls for such a dish?

BIRD. Mistress, have faith. Go now to the foot of the singing tree, dig under it and you will find what you want.

Parizade digs and finds a precious gold box filled with pearls.

PARIZADE. Parizade called the head cook to her.

Tonight you must prepare the king's favourite speciality.; cucumbers stuffed with pearls.

She opens the box.

SECOND COOK. Cucumbers stuffed with pearls?

PARIZADE. I'm surprised at you, cook. Surely you don't mean to say you've never heard of such a famously fine dish?

SECOND COOK. Really! Of course I have madam.

The cook takes the box and goes away.

Then, the princess told the servants to make ready for the visit of the King.

King's arrival. Parizade goes before him and kisses the floor.

BROTHERS. This is our sister.

The King helps her up.

KING. I hope to get to know you better, madam, after I have seen the house.

PARIZADE. So the princess showed him the golden water, singing tree, and the talking bird, who sat in his cage in the hall.

BIRD. The king is welcome here. Allah spare him and grant him a long life.

KING. Bird I thank you and am overjoyed to have found in you the King of birds.

The bird bows.

They sit down to eat..

The King reaches out and takes a cucumber.

Cucumbers stuffed with pearls? Pearls are not to be eaten! This is an affront to the royal house.

BIRD. Can your majesty be so amazed at seeing cucumbers stuffed with pearls? Yet you readily believe that the Queen, your wife, gave birth to a dog, a cat and a piece of wood.

KING. I believed it because I was told by her midwives.

BIRD. Those midwives were the Queen's wicked sisters, who out of envy and revenge lied to your majesty. Awake from your sleep of ignorance. The brothers and sister that you see before you are your own children. Found by the Steward of your Garden who brought them up and educated them as his own.

KING. My heart whispered the truth from the moment I met you.

They embrace.

And now the world shall embrace you as worthy children to the royal house of Persia.

ALL THREE. So by torchlight, they set out for the city on their horses.

KING. As soon as they reached the palace, the King ordered the Vizier to bring the Queen's envious sisters immediately to trial.

VIZIER. And after they were found guilty . . .

The two sisters hold dolls of themselves up.

SECOND. . . . . they were each cut into four pieces . . .

They tear the dolls up.

ELDEST. . . . . and fed to the dogs.

They 'eat' the dolls.

KING. In the meantime the King Khosrou Shah . . .

ALL THREE. . . . . followed by his three children . . .

BIRD. . . . . and the talking bird . . .

ALL FOUR. . . . . went to the great mosque.

The First Sister is freed from her cell.

KING. I come to plead your pardon for the wrong I have done you, and to make amends; Here is your crown, and here are two angelic princes

They bow before her.

and a heavenly princess;

She bows.

Our children.

They embrace.

QUEEN. Warm light flooded the Queen's heart when she saw her sacred children, after the darkness she had suffered for so many years.

The Story Without an Ending

Dawn.

The Palace.

SHAHRAZAD. My lord, this story shows the pain that follows, when a King acts without thinking and shuts his ears to the truth.

SHAHRAYAR. Shahrazad, even a King can loose his way. But he can find it again when the door to his heart is opened.

Pause.

DINARZAD. What story will you have for us tonight, sister?

Enter Vizier.

VIZIER. The executioner awaits your command, my lord.

SHAHRAZAD. Tonight I had planned to tell a special story. About another King who looses his way. It is called The Story Without an Ending. But I can't seem to remember it. The well of my stories has run dry. I fear I must go to the headsman.

SHAHRAYAR. The Executioner cannot act without royal decree.

SHAHRAZAD. But haven't you sworn that if the well of my stories dries up, I must die?

Silence.

Vizier, didn't you hear the King say this?

VIZIER. Well . . .

SHAHRAZAD. Didn't you?

VIZIER. I did.

SHAHRAZAD. Sister, you heard this didn't you?

DINARZAD. Yes.

SHAHRAZAD. Unless the King is not a man of his word, I must go to the executioner.

SHAHRAYAR. Curses on your impudence. Go then, imbecile.
GET OUT! Vizier see it done!

VIZIER. Yes, my lord.

*They exit. Shahrayar is alone. As he searches for things to do.
He becomes lonely and scared. Characters from the stories
visit the room. They move around him, speaking fragments
of lines from their stories. He tries to block them out.*

The hunchback stumbles past.

VIZIER FROM ENVIOUS. Laws are made to punish crimes.

Two of the dogs from Sidi Nu'uman run past.

ALI BABA. OPEN SESAME!

TALKING BIRD. I know who you really are. And I can tell
you. It is not who you think you are.

Marjanah dances by.

SINDIBAD. Till that moment I believed I would never leave
the valley alive, but now I started to see a way out.

*The rukh swirls around him. The room is full of characters.
from Shahrazad's stories.*

KING. Shahrazad! Shahrazad! Come back here! Vizier,
Headsman, Stop! Stop! STOOOOP!

The characters exit.

Shahrazad, Dinarzad, Vizier and court enter.

SHAHRAZAD. You called, your majesty.

SHAHRAYAR. Wife, if you insist on following this ridiculous
course, I shall not stand in your way.

SHAHRAZAD. Thank you your majesty.

SHAHRAYAR. I am a man of my word.

SHAHRAZAD. And a King's word is sacred, my lord.

SHAHRAYAR. But before you go, I have one last request.

SHAHRAZAD. Certainly. How may I be of help?

SHAHRAYAR. Try to remember your story. The Story Without an Ending.

SHAHRAZAD. I'll see what I can do. (*She thinks hard.*) Very Well, now. Listen . . .

Once there was a strong, brave King who loved to laugh. One day, he was betrayed by his wicked wife and lost all his love of women and his happiness. A lonely black night fell in his heart and his soul was possessed by a dark demon. 'There is not a single good woman anywhere on the face of the earth', he would cry.

Although he looked the same on the outside, on the inside, the good king of old was replaced by a cruel, merciless tyrant. Every night he would marry a different woman and the next morning, he would have her killed. This way no one could ever cheat on him again and he was safe. Darkness spread from his heart around the palace and hung heavy over the city. Many young women died. The people feared for their daughters and grew angry and confused. 'Where has our big hearted king disappeared to?' they asked.

Now the King's Vizier had two daughters and the eldest daughter was blessed with a magic power. Fate had decreed that she use this magic power to slay the dark demon in the King's soul and bring the daylight back to his world. When she saw him she knew that she was also fated to love him, with a love as true as the sky and as mysterious as the moon. This woman was called Shahrazad and her magic was the magic of stories.

Night after moonlit night, she would pour the magic medicine of her stories into his ears. And little by little, dawn started to break in his heart and a tiny flower laid its precious roots there. Before long, the daughters of the city walked freely in the sunshine. And news that the king no longer lived in darkness travelled across the land like a white horse of hope and over the sparkling sea, bathing those that heard it in warm light.

After a long, long time, the Queen found that she was expecting the king's baby. When she had told him her stories for 1001 nights, she tested the king to see if the flower in his heart had bloomed and whether he was ready to save the life of his wife and unborn child.

There the story runs out, my lord.

Shahrayar falls to his knees and cries.

SHAHRAYAR. Shahrazad, forgive me.

SHAHRAZAD. It is not me but your people you must ask to forgive you. I forgave you long ago.

SHAHRAYAR. Vizier.

VIZIER. Yes, my lord.

SHAHRAYAR. Publish in the city that King Shahrayar has lifted the death sentence on Queen Shahrazad.

VIZIER. Certainly, my lord.

SHAHRAYAR. And that she is expecting the King's baby.

VIZIER. Yes, my lord.

SHAHRAYAR. Oh and Vizier.

VIZIER. Yes, my lord.

SHAHRAYAR. Have the day off.

VIZIER. Yes, my lord.

SHAHRAYAR. Now let us celebrate the freedom of our gracious Queen.

SHAHRAZAD. And the welcome return of the good King.

She offers her hand.

They kiss.

Dance. A celebration of rebirth.

After dance. Full company join for.

EPILOGUE

ACTOR 1. Celebrations spread throughout the land . . .

ACTOR 2. . . . with eating and drinking and dancing for many days.

ACTOR 3. Afterwards, in honour of the young women who had lost their lives, the king called together his scribes and scholars . . .

ACTOR 4. . . . and ordered them to write down every one of Shahrazad's enchanting stories into a book.

ACTOR 5. One story for each of the young women . . .

ACTOR 5. . . . And one story for each night that the King's heart lived in darkness.

SHAHRAYAR. And the book lived longer than the King . . .

SHAHRAZAD. . . . and Shahrazad . . .

DINARZAD. . . . and their children . . .

ACTOR 1. . . . and their children's children,

ACTOR 2. Even the city itself.

ACTOR 3. And they called this Book Alf Layla wa Layla . . .

ACTOR 4. . . . 1001 Nights.

ACTOR 5. But even now, when the desert sky is as dark as doom . . .

ACTOR 5. . . . and the sand glows silver in the moonlight . . .

SHAHRAYAR. . . . on the site where the old city used to be . . .

DINARZAD. . . . you can hear the sweet voice of a beautiful young woman, weaving magical tales into the night.

SHAHRAZAD. Listen . . .

Lights out.

The End.

A Nick Hern Book

Arabian Nights first published in this revised edition in Great
Britain in 1999 as a paperback original by Nick Hern Books
Limited, 14 Larden Road, London W3 7ST in association with
the Young Vic Theatre, The Cut, London SE1 8LZ

Typeset by Country Setting, Kingsdown, Kent CT14 8ES
Printed and bound in Great Britain by
Cox & Wyman Ltd, Reading, Berkshire

ISBN 1 85459 461 3

A CIP catalogue record for this book is available from
the British Library